GLOBAL INITIATIVE FOR CHRONIC OBSTRUCTIVE LUNG DISEASE

POCKET GUIDE TO COPD DIAGNOSIS, MANAGEMENT, AND PREVENTION

A Guide for Health Care Professionals

2020 EDITION

ii

TABLE OF CONTENTS

GLOBAL STRATEGY FOR THE DIAGNOSIS, MANAGEMENT, AND PREVENTION OF COPD

INTRODUCTION

Chronic Obstructive Pulmonary Disease (COPD) is currently the fourth leading cause of death in the world[1] but is projected to be the 3rd leading cause of death by 2020. More than 3 million people died of COPD in 2012 accounting for 6% of all deaths globally. COPD represents an important public health challenge that is both preventable and treatable. COPD is a major cause of chronic morbidity and mortality throughout the world; many people suffer from this disease for years and die prematurely from it or its complications. Globally, the COPD burden is projected to increase in coming decades because of continued exposure to COPD risk factors and aging of the population.[2]

This Pocket Guide has been developed from the Global Strategy for the Diagnosis, Management, and Prevention of COPD (2020 Report), which aims to provide a non-biased review of the current evidence for the assessment, diagnosis and treatment of patients with COPD that can aid the clinician. Discussions of COPD and COPD management, evidence levels, and specific citations from the scientific literature are included in that source document, which is available from www.goldcopd.org.

DEFINITION AND OVERVIEW

OVERALL KEY POINTS:

• *Chronic Obstructive Pulmonary Disease (COPD) is a common, preventable and treatable disease that is characterized by persistent respiratory symptoms and airflow limitation that is due to airway and/or alveolar abnormalities usually caused by significant exposure to noxious particles or gases.*

• *The most common respiratory symptoms include dyspnea, cough and/or sputum production. These symptoms may be under-reported by patients.*

• *The main risk factor for COPD is tobacco smoking but other environmental exposures such as biomass fuel exposure and air pollution may contribute. Besides exposures, host factors predispose individuals to develop COPD. These include genetic abnormalities, abnormal lung development and accelerated aging.*

• *COPD may be punctuated by periods of acute worsening of respiratory symptoms, called exacerbations.*

• *In most patients, COPD is associated with significant concomitant chronic diseases, which increase its morbidity and mortality.*

WHAT IS CHRONIC OBSTRUCTIVE PULMONARY DISEASE (COPD)?

Chronic Obstructive Pulmonary Disease (COPD) is a common, preventable and treatable disease that is characterized by persistent respiratory symptoms and airflow limitation that is due to airway and/or alveolar abnormalities usually caused by significant exposure to noxious particles or gases and influenced by host factors including abnormal lung development. Significant comorbidities may have an impact on morbidity and mortality. There may be significant lung pathology (e.g., emphysema) in the absence of airflow limitation that needs further evaluation (**see Figure**).

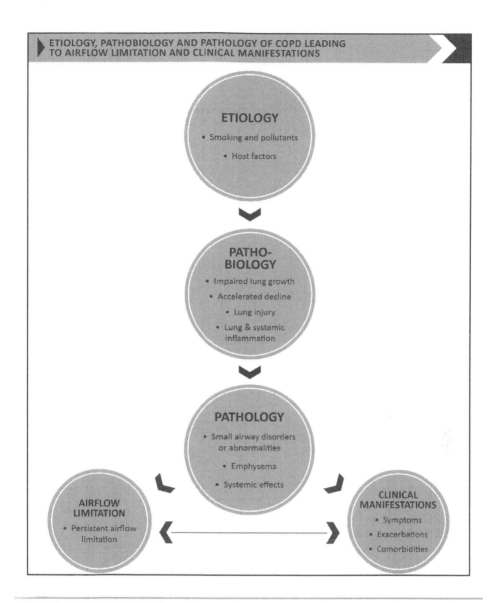

WHAT CAUSES COPD?

Worldwide, the most commonly encountered risk factor for COPD is **tobacco smoking**. Nonsmokers may also develop COPD. COPD is the result of a complex interplay of long-term cumulative exposure to noxious gases and particles, combined with a variety of host factors including genetics, airway hyper-responsiveness and poor lung growth during childhood.[3-5] The risk of developing COPD is related to the following factors:

- **Tobacco smoke** – cigarette smokers have a higher prevalence of respiratory symptoms and lung function abnormalities, a greater annual rate of decline in FEV_1, and a greater COPD mortality rate than non-smokers.[6] Other types of tobacco (e.g., pipe, cigar, water pipe)[7-9] and marijuana[10] are also risk factors for COPD, as well as environmental tobacco smoke (ETS). [11]

- **Indoor air pollution** – resulting from the burning of wood and other biomass fuels used for cooking and heating in poorly vented dwellings, is a risk factor that particularly affects women in developing countries. [12,13]

- **Occupational exposures** – including organic and inorganic dusts, chemical agents and fumes, are under-appreciated risk factors for COPD. [12,14]

- **Outdoor air pollution** – also contributes to the lungs' total burden of inhaled particles, although it appears to have a relatively small effect in causing COPD.

- **Genetic factors** – such as severe hereditary deficiency of alpha-1 antitrypsin (AATD) [15]; the gene encoding matrix metalloproteinase 12 (*MMP-12*) and glutathione *S*-transferase have also been related to a decline in lung function[16] or risk of COPD.[17]

- **Age and sex** – aging and female sex increase COPD risk.

- **Lung growth and development** – any factor that affects lung growth during gestation and childhood (low birth weight, respiratory infections, etc.) has the potential to increase an individual's risk of developing COPD.

- **Socioeconomic status** – Poverty is consistently associated with airflow obstruction[18] and lower socioeconomic status is associated with an increased risk of developing COPD.[19,20] It is not clear, however, whether this pattern reflects exposures to indoor and outdoor air pollutants, crowding, poor nutrition, infections, or other factors related to low socioeconomic status.

- **Asthma and airway hyper-reactivity** – asthma may be a risk factor for the development of airflow limitation and COPD.

- **Chronic bronchitis** – may increase the frequency of total and severe exacerbations.[21]

- **Infections** – a history of severe childhood respiratory infection has been associated with reduced lung function and increased respiratory symptoms in adulthood. [22]

DIAGNOSIS AND ASSESSMENT OF COPD

OVERALL KEY POINTS:

• *COPD should be considered in any patient who has dyspnea, chronic cough or sputum production, a history of recurrent lower respiratory tract infections and/or a history of exposure to risk factors for the disease.*

• *Spirometry is required to make the diagnosis; the presence of a post-bronchodilator $FEV_1/FVC < 0.70$*

> *confirms the presence of persistent airflow limitation.*
>
> • *The goals of COPD assessment are to determine the level of airflow limitation, the impact of disease on the patient's health status, and the risk of future events (such as exacerbations, hospital admissions, or death), in order to guide therapy.*
>
> • *Concomitant chronic diseases occur frequently in COPD patients, including cardiovascular disease, skeletal muscle dysfunction, metabolic syndrome, osteoporosis, depression, anxiety, and lung cancer. These comorbidities should be actively sought and treated appropriately when present as they can influence mortality and hospitalizations independently.*

DIAGNOSIS

COPD should be considered in any patient who has dyspnea, chronic cough or sputum production, and/or a history of exposure to risk factors for the disease (**see Table**). Spirometry is required to make the diagnosis in this clinical context[23]; the presence of a post-bronchodilator $FEV_1/FVC < 0.70$ confirms the presence of persistent airflow limitation and thus of COPD in patients with appropriate symptoms and significant exposures to noxious stimuli. Spirometry is the most reproducible and objective measurement of airflow limitation. It is a noninvasive and readily available test. Despite its good sensitivity, peak expiratory flow measurement alone cannot be reliably used as the only diagnostic test because of its weak specificity.[24]

DIFFERENTIAL DIAGNOSIS

A major differential diagnosis is asthma. In some patients with chronic asthma, a clear distinction from COPD is not possible using current imaging and physiological testing techniques. In these patients, current management is similar to that of asthma. Other potential diagnoses are usually easier to distinguish from COPD (**see Table**).

Alpha-1 antitrypsin deficiency (AATD) screening. The World Health Organization recommends that all patients with a diagnosis of COPD should be screened once especially in areas with high AATD prevalence.[25] A low concentration (< 20% normal) is highly suggestive of homozygous deficiency. Family members should also be screened.

Additional investigations

The following additional investigations may be considered as part of the diagnosis and assessment of COPD.

Imaging. A chest X-ray is not useful to establish a diagnosis in COPD, but it is valuable in excluding alternative diagnoses and establishing the presence of significant comorbidities such as concomitant respiratory (pulmonary fibrosis, bronchiectasis, pleural diseases), skeletal (e.g., kyphoscoliosis), and cardiac diseases (e.g., cardiomegaly). Radiological changes associated with COPD include signs of lung hyperinflation (flattened diaphragm and an increase in the volume of the retrosternal air space), hyperlucency of the lungs, and rapid tapering of the vascular markings. Computed tomography (CT) of the chest is not routinely recommended except for detection of bronchiectasis and COPD patients that meet the criteria for lung cancer risk assessment. The presence of emphysema in particular may increase the risk for development of lung cancer. However, CT scanning may be helpful in the differential diagnosis where concomitant diseases are present. In addition, if a surgical procedure such as lung volume reduction,[26] or increasingly non-surgical based lung volume reduction[27] is contemplated, a chest CT scan is necessary since the distribution of emphysema is one of the most important determinants of surgical suitability. A CT scan is also required for patients being evaluated for lung transplantation.

4

Lung volumes and diffusing capacity. COPD patients exhibit gas trapping (a rise in residual volume) from the early stages of the disease, and as airflow limitation worsens, static hyperinflation (an increase in total lung capacity) occurs. These changes can be documented by body plethysmography, or less accurately by helium dilution lung volume measurement. These measurements help characterize the severity of COPD but are not essential to patient management. Measurement of diffusing capacity (DLCO) provides information on the functional impact of emphysema in COPD and is often helpful in patients with breathlessness that may seem out of proportion to the degree of airflow limitation.

Oximetry and arterial blood gas measurement. Pulse oximetry can be used to evaluate a patient's arterial oxygen saturation and need for supplemental oxygen therapy. Pulse oximetry should be used to assess all patients with clinical signs suggestive of respiratory failure or right heart failure. If peripheral arterial oxygen saturation is < 92% arterial or capillary blood gases should be assessed.[28,29]

Exercise testing and assessment of physical activity. Objectively measured exercise impairment, assessed by a reduction in self-paced walking distance[30,31] or during incremental exercise testing in a laboratory,[32] is a powerful indicator of health status impairment and predictor of prognosis; exercise capacity may fall in the year before death.[33] Walking tests can be useful for assessing disability and risk of mortality[34] and are used to assess the effectiveness of pulmonary rehabilitation. Both the paced shuttle walk test[35] and the unpaced 6-minute walk test can be used.[36,37] As the course length has a substantial impact on the distance walked, existing reference equations established for a 30 meter course cannot be applied to predict the distance achieved on shorter courses.[38] Laboratory testing using cycle or treadmill ergometry can assist in identifying co-existing or alternative conditions e.g., cardiac diagnoses.

▶ KEY INDICATORS FOR CONSIDERING A DIAGNOSIS OF COPD

Consider COPD, and perform spirometry, if any of these indicators are present in an individual over age 40. These indicators are not diagnostic themselves, but the presence of multiple key indicators increases the probability of a diagnosis of COPD. Spirometry is required to establish a diagnosis of COPD.

Dyspnea that is:	Progressive over time. Characteristically worse with exercise. Persistent.
Chronic Cough:	May be intermittent and may be unproductive. Recurrent wheeze.
Chronic Sputum Production:	Any pattern of chronic sputum production may indicate COPD.
Recurrent Lower Respiratory Tract Infections	
History of Risk Factors:	Host factors (such as genetic factors, congenital/developmental abnormalities etc.). Tobacco smoke (including popular local preparations). Smoke from home cooking and heating fuels. Occupational dusts, vapors, fumes, gases and other chemicals.
Family History of COPD and/or Childhood Factors:	For example low birthweight, childhood respiratory infections etc.

Monitoring of physical activity may be more relevant regarding prognosis than evaluating exercise capacity.[39] This can be conducted using accelerometers or multi-sensor instruments.

Composite scores. Several variables identify patients at increased risk for mortality including FEV_1, exercise tolerance assessed by walking distance or peak oxygen consumption, weight loss, and reduction in arterial oxygen tension. A relatively simple approach to identifying disease severity using a combination of most of the above variables has been proposed. The BODE (Body mass index, Obstruction, Dyspnea, and Exercise) method gives a composite score that is a better predictor of subsequent survival than any single component.[40,41] Simpler alternatives that do not include an exercise test have been suggested but all these approaches need validation across a wide range of disease severities and clinical settings to confirm that they are suitable for routine clinical use.[42,43]

Differential diagnoses. In some patients with chronic asthma, a clear distinction from COPD is difficult using current imaging and physiological testing techniques, since the two conditions share common traits and clinical expressions. Most other potential differential diagnoses are easier to distinguish from COPD (**Table 2.7**).

Biomarkers. There is rapidly increasing interest in the use of biomarkers in COPD. Biomarkers are 'characteristics that are objectively measured and evaluated as an indicator of normal biological or pathogenic processes or pharmacological responses to therapeutic interventions'. In general such data has proven difficult to interpret, largely as a result of weak associations and lack of reproducibility between large patient cohorts[44] which was further confirmed in the recent SUMMIT study.[45] Recent studies (see **Chapter 5** - Exacerbations) have indicated the use of C-reactive protein (CRP) and procalcitonin[46] in restricting antibiotic usage during exacerbations, although the observed sputum color remains highly sensitive and specific for a high bacterial load during such episodes.

At present the assessment of eosinophils provides the best guidance to the use of corticosteroids[44] especially in the prevention of some exacerbations (see **Chapter 3** - Inhaled Corticosteroids). Continued cautious and realistic interpretation of the role of biomarkers in the management of identified clinical traits is required.

Other considerations. It is clear that some patients *without evidence of airflow limitation* have evidence of structural lung disease on chest imaging (emphysema, gas trapping, airway wall thickening) that is consistent with what is found in patients with COPD. Such patients may report exacerbations of respiratory symptoms or even require treatment with respiratory medications on a chronic basis. Whether these patients have acute or chronic bronchitis, a persistent form of asthma or an earlier presentation of what will become COPD as it is currently defined, is unclear at present and will require further study.

DIAGNOSIS	SUGGESTIVE FEATURES
COPD	Onset in mid-life. Symptoms slowly progressive. History of tobacco smoking or exposure to other types of smoke.
Asthma	Onset early in life (often childhood). Symptoms vary widely from day to day. Symptoms worse at night/early morning. Allergy, rhinitis, and/or eczema also present. Family history of asthma. Obesity coexistence.
Congestive Heart Failure	Chest X-ray shows dilated heart, pulmonary edema. Pulmonary function tests indicate volume restriction, not airflow limitation.
Bronchiectasis	Large volumes of purulent sputum. Commonly associated with bacterial infection. Chest X-ray/CT shows bronchial dilation, bronchial wall thickening.
Tuberculosis	Onset all ages. Chest X-ray shows lung infiltrate. Microbiological confirmation. High local prevalence of tuberculosis.
Obliterative Bronchiolitis	Onset at younger age, nonsmokers. May have history of rheumatoid arthritis or acute fume exposure. Seen after lung or bone marrow transplantation. CT on expiration shows hypodense areas.
Diffuse Panbronchiolitis	Predominantly seen in patients of Asian descent. Most patients are male and nonsmokers. Almost all have chronic sinusitis. Chest X-ray & HRCT show diffuse small centrilobular nodular opacities & hyperinflation.

These features tend to be characteristic of the respective diseases, but are not mandatory. For example, a person who has never smoked may develop COPD (especially in the developing world where other risk factors may be more important than cigarette smoking); asthma may develop in adult and even in elderly patients.

ASSESSMENT

The goals of COPD assessment are to determine the level of airflow limitation, its impact on the patient's health status and the risk of future events (such as exacerbations, hospital admissions or death), in order to, eventually, guide therapy. To achieve these goals, COPD assessment must consider the following aspects of the disease separately:

- ▷ The presence and severity of the spirometric abnormality
- ▷ Current nature and magnitude of the patient's symptoms
- ▷ History of moderate and severe exacerbations
- ▷ Presence of comorbidities

Classification of severity of airflow limitation

The classification of airflow limitation severity in COPD (**see Table**) uses specific spirometric cut-points for purposes of simplicity. Spirometry should be performed after the administration of an adequate dose of at least one short-acting inhaled bronchodilator in order to minimize variability.

It should be noted that there is only a weak correlation between FEV_1, symptoms and impairment of a patient's health status.[47,48] For this reason, formal symptomatic assessment is required.

CLASSIFICATION OF AIRFLOW LIMITATION SEVERITY IN COPD (BASED ON POST-BRONCHODILATOR FEV_1)		
In patients with FEV1/FVC < 0.70:		
GOLD 1:	Mild	$FEV_1 \geq 80\%$ predicted
GOLD 2:	Moderate	$50\% \leq FEV_1 < 80\%$ predicted
GOLD 3:	Severe	$30\% \leq FEV_1 < 50\%$ predicted
GOLD 4:	Very Severe	$FEV_1 < 30\%$ predicted

Assessment of symptoms

In the past, COPD was viewed as a disease largely characterized by breathlessness. A simple measure of breathlessness such as the Modified British Medical Research Council (mMRC) Questionnaire[49] (**see Table**) was considered adequate for assessment of symptoms, as the mMRC relates well to other measures of health status[50] and predicts future mortality risk.[51,52] However, it is now recognized that COPD impacts patients beyond just dyspnea.[53] For this reason, a comprehensive assessment of symptoms is recommended using measures such as the COPD Assessment Test (CAT™)[54] (**see Figure**) and The COPD Control Questionnaire (The CCQ©).

MODIFIED MRC DYSPNEA SCALE[a]

mMRC Grade 0.	I only get breathless with strenuous exercise.	☐
mMRC Grade 1.	I get short of breath when hurrying on the level or walking up a slight hill.	☐
mMRC Grade 2.	I walk slower than people of the same age on the level because of breathlessness, or I have to stop for breath when walking on my own pace on the level.	☐
mMRC Grade 3.	I stop for breath after walking about 100 meters or after a few minutes on the level.	☐
mMRC Grade 4.	I am too breathless to leave the house or I am breathless when dressing or undressing.	☐

[a] Fletcher CM. BMJ 1960; 2: 1662.

CAT™ ASSESSMENT

For each item below, place a mark (x) in the box that best describes you currently. Be sure to only select one response for each question.

		SCORE
EXAMPLE: I am very happy	(0) (☒) (2) (3) (4) (5) I am very sad	
I never cough	(0) (1) (2) (3) (4) (5) I cough all the time	
I have no phlegm (mucus) in my chest at all	(0) (1) (2) (3) (4) (5) My chest is completely full of phlegm (mucus)	
My chest does not feel tight at all	(0) (1) (2) (3) (4) (5) My chest feels very tight	
When I walk up a hill or one flight of stairs I am not breathless	(0) (1) (2) (3) (4) (5) When I walk up a hill or one flight of stairs I am very breathless	
I am not limited doing any activities at home	(0) (1) (2) (3) (4) (5) I am very limited doing activities at home	
I am confident leaving my home despite my lung condition	(0) (1) (2) (3) (4) (5) I am not at all confident leaving my home because of my lung condition	
I sleep soundly	(0) (1) (2) (3) (4) (5) I don't sleep soundly because of my lung condition	
I have lots of energy	(0) (1) (2) (3) (4) (5) I have no energy at all	

Reference: Jones et al. ERJ 2009; 34 (3); 648-54.

TOTAL SCORE: ◯

Combined COPD assessment

An understanding of the impact of COPD on an individual patient combines the symptomatic assessment with the patient's spirometric classification and/or risk of exacerbations. The "ABCD" assessment tool of the 2011 GOLD update was a major step forward from the simple spirometric grading system of the earlier versions of GOLD because it incorporated patient-reported outcomes and highlighted the importance of exacerbation prevention in the management of COPD. However, there were some important limitations. Firstly, the ABCD assessment tool performed no better than the spirometric grades for mortality prediction or other important health outcomes in COPD.[55-57] Moreover, group "D" outcomes were modified by two parameters: lung function and/or exacerbation history, which caused confusion.[48] To address these and other concerns (while at the same time maintaining consistency and simplicity for the practicing clinician), a refinement of the ABCD assessment tool is proposed that separates spirometric grades from the "ABCD" groups. For some therapeutic recommendations, ABCD groups are derived exclusively from patient symptoms and their history of exacerbation. Spirometry, in conjunction with patient symptoms and history of moderate and severe exacerbations, remains vital for the diagnosis, prognostication and consideration of other important therapeutic approaches. This new approach to assessment is illustrated in the **Figure**.

In the revised assessment scheme, patients should undergo spirometry to determine the severity of airflow limitation (i.e., spirometric grade). They should also undergo assessment of either dyspnea using mMRC or symptoms using CAT™. Finally, their history of moderate and severe exacerbations (including prior hospitalizations) should be recorded.

The number provides information regarding severity of airflow limitation (spirometric grade 1 to 4) while the letter (groups A to D) provides information regarding symptom burden and risk of exacerbation which can be used to guide therapy. FEV_1 is a very important parameter at the population-level in the prediction of important clinical outcomes such as mortality and hospitalizations or prompting consideration for non-pharmacological therapies such as lung volume reduction or lung transplantation. However, it is important to note that at the individual patient level, FEV_1 loses precision and thus cannot be used alone to determine all therapeutic options. Furthermore, in some circumstances, such as during hospitalization or urgent presentation to the clinic or emergency room, the ability to assess patients based on symptoms and exacerbation history, independent of the spirometric value, allows clinicians to initiate a treatment plan based on the revised ABCD scheme alone. This assessment approach acknowledges the limitations of FEV_1 in making treatment decisions for individualized patient care and highlights the importance of patient symptoms and exacerbation risks in guiding therapies in COPD. The separation of airflow limitation from clinical parameters makes it clearer what is being evaluated and ranked. This facilitates more precise treatment recommendations based on parameters that are driving the patient's symptoms at any given time.

THE REFINED ABCD ASSESSMENT TOOL

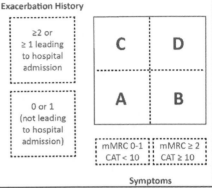

| Spirometrically Confirmed Diagnosis | » | Assessment of airflow limitation | » | Assessment of symptoms/risk of exacerbations |

| Post-bronchodilator FEV₁/FVC < 0.7 |

Moderate or Severe Exacerbation History

Grade	FEV₁ (% predicted)
GOLD 1	≥ 80
GOLD 2	50-79
GOLD 3	30-49
GOLD 4	< 30

≥2 or ≥ 1 leading to hospital admission

0 or 1 (not leading to hospital admission)

C	D
A	B

| mMRC 0-1 CAT < 10 | mMRC ≥ 2 CAT ≥ 10 |

Symptoms

Example: Consider two patients - both patients with FEV₁ < 30% of predicted, CAT™ scores of 18 and one with no exacerbations in the past year and the other with three moderate exacerbations in the past year. Both would have been labelled GOLD D in the prior classification scheme. However, with the new proposed scheme, the subject with three moderate exacerbations in the past year would be labelled GOLD grade 4, group D.

The role of spirometry for the diagnosis, assessment and follow-up of COPD is summarized in the **Table.**

ROLE OF SPIROMETRY

- **Diagnosis**

- **Assessment of severity of airflow obstruction (for prognosis)**

- **Follow-up assessment**

    » Therapeutic decisions.

        – Pharmacological in selected circumstances (e.g., discrepancy between spirometry and level of symptoms).

        – Consider alternative diagnoses when symptoms are disproportionate to degree of airflow obstruction.

        – Non-pharmacological (e.g., interventional procedures).

    » Identification of rapid decline.

EVIDENCE SUPPORTING PREVENTION AND MAINTENANCE THERAPY

OVERALL KEY POINTS:

• *Smoking cessation is key. Pharmacotherapy and nicotine replacement reliably increase long-term smoking abstinence rates. Legislative smoking bans and counselling, delivered by healthcare professionals improve quit rates.*

• *The effectiveness and safety of e-cigarettes as a smoking cessation aid is uncertain at present.*

• *Pharmacological therapy can reduce COPD symptoms, reduce the frequency and severity of exacerbations, and improve health status and exercise tolerance.*

• *Each pharmacological treatment regimen should be individualized and guided by the severity of symptoms, risk of exacerbations, side-effects, comorbidities, drug availability and cost, and the patient's response, preference and ability to use various drug delivery devices.*

• *Inhaler technique needs to be assessed regularly.*

• *Influenza vaccination decreases the incidence of lower respiratory tract infections.*

• *Pneumococcal vaccination decreases lower respiratory tract infections.*

• *Pulmonary rehabilitation improves symptoms, quality of life, and physical and emotional participation in everyday activities.*

• *In patients with severe resting chronic hypoxemia, long-term oxygen therapy improves survival.*

• *In patients with stable COPD and resting or exercise-induced moderate desaturation, long-term oxygen treatment should not be prescribed routinely. However, individual patient factors must be considered when evaluating the patient's need for supplemental oxygen.*

• *In patients with severe chronic hypercapnia and a history of hospitalization for acute respiratory failure, long-term non-invasive ventilation may decrease mortality and prevent re-hospitalization.*

• *In select patients with advanced emphysema refractory to optimized medical care, surgical or bronchoscopic interventional treatments may be beneficial.*

• *Palliative approaches are effective in controlling symptoms in advanced COPD.*

SMOKING CESSATION

Smoking cessation has the greatest capacity to influence the natural history of COPD. If effective resources and time are dedicated to smoking cessation, long-term quit success rates of up to 25% can be achieved.[58] Besides individual approaches to smoking cessation, legislative smoking bans are effective in increasing quit rates and reducing harm from second-hand smoke exposure.[59] A five-step program for intervention (**see Table**)[60-62] provides a helpful strategic framework.[60,62,63]

E-cigarettes were originally promoted as a form of nicotine replacement therapy to aid in smoking cessation, although the efficacy to aid smoking cessation remains controversial.[64,65] Tetrahydrocannabinol (THC), cannabinoid (CBD) oils, Vitamin E and other flavoring substances and additives have been added to nicotine and promoted to previously non-smoking adolescents and young adults (also known as vaping). Severe acute lung injury, eosinophilic pneumonia, alveolar hemorrhage, respiratory bronchiolitis and other forms of lung abnormalities have been reportedly linked to E-cigarette use.[66-69]

Recently, the U.S. Centers for Disease Control (CDC), the U.S. Food and Drug Administration (FDA), state and other clinical and public health partners are investigating outbreaks of lung illness associated with e-cigarette product use (devices, liquids, refill pods, and/or cartridges). As of October 22, 2019, 1,604 cases of lung illness and 34 deaths have been associated with using e-cigarette products.[69] All patients had reported a history of using e-cigarette, or vaping products and most reported a history of using THC-containing products. These latest findings suggest that products containing THC, particularly those obtained off the street or from unofficial sources (e.g., friends, family members, illicit dealers), are linked to most of the cases in the outbreak.[69] In a case cohort analysis, no evidence of infection was found, lung inflammation and injury was evident.[69] Patients were reported to have had clinical improvement with systemic glucocorticoid therapy and the majority received prolonged courses; specific clinical recommendations are not available at this time.[68]

▶ BRIEF STRATEGIES TO HELP THE PATIENT WILLING TO QUIT

• **ASK:**	Systematically identify all tobacco users at every visit. *Implement an office-wide system that ensures that, for EVERY patient at EVERY clinic visit, tobacco-use status is queried and documented.*
• **ADVISE:**	Strongly urge all tobacco users to quit. *In a clear, strong, and personalized manner, urge every tobacco user to quit.*
• **ASSESS:**	Determine willingness and rationale of patient's desire to make a quit attempt. *Ask every tobacco user if he or she is willing to make a quit attempt at this time (e.g., within the next 30 days).*
• **ASSIST:**	Aid the patient in quitting. *Help the patient with a quit plan; provide practical counseling; provide intra-treatment social support; help the patient obtain extra-treatment social support; recommend use of approved pharmacotherapy except in special circumstances; provide supplementary materials.*
• **ARRANGE:**	Schedule follow-up contact. *Schedule follow-up contact, either in person or via telephone.*

VACCINATIONS

▶ VACCINATION FOR STABLE COPD

- Influenza vaccination reduces serious illness and death in COPD patients **(EvidenceB)**.

- The 23-valent pneumococcal polysaccharide vaccine (PPSV23) has been shown to reduce the incidence of community - acquired pneumonia in COPD patients aged < 65 years with an FEV_1 < 40% predicted and in those with comorbidities **(Evidence B)**.

- In the general population of adults ≥65 years the 13-valent conjugated pneumococcal vaccine (PCV13) has demonstrated significant efficacy in reducing bacteremia & serious invasive pneumococcal disease **(Evidence B)**.

COMMONLY USED MAINTENANCE MEDICATIONS IN COPD*

| Generic Drug Name | Inhaler Type | DELIVERY OPTIONS | | | Duration Of Action |
		Nebulizer	Oral	Injection	
BETA₂-AGONISTS					
SHORT-ACTING (SABA)					
Fenoterol	MDI	√	pill, syrup		4-6 hours
Levalbuterol	MDI	√			6-8 hours
Salbutamol (albuterol)	MDI & DPI	√	pill, syrup, extended release tablet	√	4-6 hours / 12 hours (ext. release)
Terbutaline	DPI		pill	√	4-6 hours
LONG-ACTING (LABA)					
Arformoterol		√			12 hours
Formoterol	DPI	√			12 hours
Indacaterol	DPI				24 hours
Olodaterol	SMI				24 hours
Salmeterol	MDI & DPI				12 hours
ANTICHOLINERGICS					
SHORT-ACTING (SAMA)					
Ipratropium bromide	MDI	√			6-8 hours
Oxitropium bromide	MDI				7-9 hours
LONG-ACTING (LAMA)					
Aclidinium bromide	DPI, MDI				12 hours
Glycopyrronium bromide	DPI		solution	√	12-24 hours
Tiotropium	DPI, SMI, MDI				24 hours
Umeclidinium	DPI				24 hours
Glycopyrrolate		√			12 hours
Revefenacin		√			24 hours
COMBINATION SHORT-ACTING BETA₂-AGONIST PLUS ANTICHOLINERGIC IN ONE DEVICE (SABA/SAMA)					
Fenoterol/ipratropium	SMI	√			6-8 hours
Salbutamol/ipratropium	SMI, MDI	√			6-8 hours
COMBINATION LONG-ACTING BETA₂-AGONIST PLUS ANTICHOLINERGIC IN ONE DEVICE (LABA/LAMA)					
Formoterol/aclidinium	DPI				12 hours
Formoterol/glycopyrronium	MDI				12 hours
Indacaterol/glycopyrronium	DPI				12-24 hours
Vilanterol/umeclidinium	DPI				24 hours
Olodaterol/tiotropium	SMI				24 hours
METHYLXANTHINES					
Aminophylline			solution	√	Variable, up to 24 hours
Theophylline (SR)			pill	√	Variable, up to 24 hours
COMBINATION OF LONG-ACTING BETA₂-AGONIST PLUS CORTICOSTEROID IN ONE DEVICE (LABA/ICS)					
Formoterol/beclometasone	MDI, DPI				12 hours
Formoterol/budesonide	MDI, DPI				12 hours
Formoterol/mometasone	MDI				12 hours
Salmeterol/fluticasone	MDI, DPI				12 hours
Vilanterol/fluticasone furoate	DPI				24 hours
TRIPLE COMBINATION IN ONE DEVICE (LABA/LAMA/ICS)					
Fluticasone/umeclidinium/vilanterol	DPI				24 hours
Beclometasone/formoterol/glycopyrronium	MDI				12 hours
PHOSPHODIESTERASE-4 INHIBITORS					
Roflumilast			pill		24 hours
MUCOLYTIC AGENTS					
Erdosteine			pill		12 hours
Carbocysteine†			pill		
N-acetylcysteine†			pill		

TABLE 3.3 *Not all formulations are available in all countries. In some countries other formulations and dosages may be available. † Dosing regimens are under discussion. MDI = metered dose inhaler; DPI = dry powder inhaler; SMI = soft mist inhaler.

PHARMACOLOGICAL THERAPY FOR STABLE COPD

Overview of the medications

Pharmacological therapy for COPD is used to reduce symptoms, reduce the frequency and severity of exacerbations, and improve exercise tolerance and health status. The classes of medications commonly used to treat COPD are shown in the **Table**. To date, there is no conclusive clinical trial evidence that any existing medications for COPD modify the long-term decline in lung function.[70-74] *Post-hoc* evidence of such an effect with long-acting bronchodilators and/or inhaled corticosteroids[75,76] requires confirmation in specifically designed trials.

Bronchodilators

Bronchodilators are medications that increase FEV_1 and/or change other spirometric variables.
- Bronchodilator medications in COPD are most often given on a regular basis to prevent or reduce symptoms.
- Toxicity is also dose-related.
- Use of short acting bronchodilators on a regular basis is not generally recommended.

Beta₂-agonists
- The principal action of beta₂-agonists is to relax airway smooth muscle by stimulating beta₂-adrenergic receptors, which increases cyclic AMP and produces functional antagonism to bronchoconstriction.
- There are short-acting (SABA) and long-acting (LABA) beta₂-agonists. The effect of SABAs usually wears off within 4 to 6 hours.[77,78] Regular and as-needed use of SABAs improve FEV_1 and symptoms.[79]
- For single-dose, as-needed use in COPD, there appears to be no advantage in routinely using levalbuterol over conventional bronchodilators.[80] LABAs show duration of action of 12 or more hours and do not preclude additional benefit from as-needed SABA therapy.[81]
- Formoterol and salmeterol are twice-daily LABAs that significantly improve FEV_1 and lung volumes, dyspnea, health status, exacerbation rate and number of hospitalizations,[82] but have no effect on mortality or rate of decline of lung function.
- Indacaterol is a once daily LABA that improves breathlessness,[83,84] health status[84] and exacerbation rate.[84] Some patients experience cough following the inhalation of indacaterol.
- Oladaterol and vilanterol are additional once daily LABAs that improve lung function and symptoms.[85,86]

Adverse effects. Stimulation of beta₂-adrenergic receptors can produce resting sinus tachycardia and has the potential to precipitate cardiac rhythm disturbances in susceptible patients. Exaggerated somatic tremor is troublesome in some older patients treated with higher doses of beta₂-agonists, regardless of route of administration. Although hypokalemia can occur, especially when treatment is combined with thiazide diuretics,[87] and oxygen consumption can be increased under resting conditions in patients with chronic heart failure,[88] these metabolic effects decrease over time (i.e., show tachyphylaxis). Mild falls in partial pressure of oxygen (PaO_2) can occur after administration of both SABAs and LABAs[89] but the clinical significance of these changes is uncertain. Despite prior concerns related to the use of beta₂-agonists in the management of asthma, no association between beta₂-agonist use and loss of lung function or increased mortality has been reported in COPD.[82,90,91]

Antimuscarinic drugs
- Antimuscarinic drugs block the bronchoconstrictor effects of acetylcholine on M3 muscarinic receptors expressed in airway smooth muscle.[92]
- Short-acting antimuscarinics (SAMAs), namely ipratropium and oxitropium, also block the inhibitory neuronal receptor M2, which potentially can cause vagally induced bronchoconstriction.[93]
- Long-acting antimuscarinic antagonists (LAMAs), such as tiotropium, aclidinium, glycopyrronium bromide and umeclidinium have prolonged binding to M3 muscarinic receptors, with faster dissociation from M2

muscarinic receptors, thus prolonging the duration of bronchodilator effect.[92]

▷ A systematic review of randomized controlled trials concluded that ipratropium, a short acting muscarinic antagonist, alone provided small benefits over short-acting beta$_2$-agonist in terms of lung function, health status and requirement for oral steroids.[94]

▷ LAMA treatments (tiotropium) improve symptoms and health status.[92,95] They also improve the effectiveness of pulmonary rehabilitation[96,97] and reduce exacerbations and related hospitalizations.[95]

▷ Clinical trials have shown a greater effect on exacerbation rates for LAMA treatment (tiotropium) versus LABA treatment.[98,99]

Adverse effects. Inhaled anticholinergic drugs are poorly absorbed which limits the troublesome systemic effects observed with atropine.[92,100] Extensive use of this class of agents in a wide range of doses and clinical settings has shown them to be very safe. The main side effect is dryness of mouth.[93,101] Although occasional urinary symptoms have been reported, there are no data to prove a true causal relationship.[102] Some patients using ipratropium report a bitter, metallic taste. An unexpected small increase in cardiovascular events in COPD patients regularly treated with ipratropium bromide has been reported.[103,104] In a large, long-term clinical trial in COPD patients, tiotropium added to other standard therapies had no effect on cardiovascular risk.[74] Although there were some initial concerns regarding the safety of tiotropium delivery via the Respimat®[105] inhaler, the findings of a large trial observed no difference in mortality or exacerbation rates when comparing tiotropium in a dry-powder inhaler and the Respimat® inhaler.[106]

Methylxanthines

▷ Controversy remains about the exact effects of xanthine derivatives.

▷ Theophylline, the most commonly used methylxanthine, is metabolized by cytochrome P450 mixed function oxidases. Clearance of the drug declines with age.

▷ There is evidence for a modest bronchodilator effect compared with placebo in stable COPD.[107]

▷ Addition of theophylline to salmeterol produces a greater improvement in FEV$_1$ and breathlessness than salmeterol alone.[108,109]

▷ There is limited and contradictory evidence regarding the effect of low-dose theophylline on exacerbation rates.[110,111]

Adverse effects. Toxicity is dose-related, which is a particular problem with xanthine derivatives because their therapeutic ratio is small and most of the benefit occurs only when near-toxic doses are given.[107,112]

Combination bronchodilator therapy

Combining bronchodilators with different mechanisms and durations of action may increase the degree of bronchodilation with a lower risk of side-effects compared to increasing the dose of a single bronchodilator.[113] Combinations of SABAs and SAMAs are superior compared to either medication alone in improving FEV$_1$ and symptoms.[114] Treatment with formoterol and tiotropium in *separate inhalers* has a bigger impact on FEV$_1$ than either component alone.[115] There are numerous combinations of a LABA and LAMA in a *single inhaler* available. These combinations improve lung function compared to placebo[113]; this improvement is consistently greater than long acting bronchodilator monotherapy effects although the magnitude of improvement is less than the fully additive effect predicted by the individual component responses.[116] In studies where patient reported outcomes (PROs) are the primary endpoint or in pooled analyses, combination bronchodilators have a greater impact on PROs compared to monotherapies.[117-120] In one clinical trial, combination LABA/LAMA treatment had the greatest improvement in quality of life compare to placebo or its individual bronchodilator components in patients with a greater baseline symptom burden.[121] These clinical trials deal with group mean data, but symptom responses to LABA/LAMA combinations are best evaluated on an individual patient basis. A lower dose, twice daily regimen for a LABA/LAMA has also been shown to improve symptoms and health status in COPD patients[122] (**see Table**). These findings have been shown in people across different ethnic groups (Asian as well as European).[123]

Most studies with LABA/LAMA combinations have been performed in patients with a low rate of exacerbations. One study in patients with a history of exacerbations indicated that a combination of long-acting bronchodilators is more effective than long-acting bronchodilator monotherapy for preventing exacerbations.[124] Another large study found that combining a LABA with a LAMA did not reduce exacerbation rate as much as expected compared with a LAMA alone.[125] Another study in patients with a history of exacerbations confirmed that a combination LABA/LAMA decreased exacerbations to a greater extent than an ICS/LABA combination.[126] However, another study in a population with high exacerbation risk (≥ 2 exacerbations and/or 1 hospitalization in the previous year) reported that ICS/LABA decreased exacerbations to a greater extent than an LABA/LAMA combination at higher blood eosinophil concentrations.[127] A large observational pharmaco-epidemiological study found similar effectiveness of LABA/LAMA and ICS/LABA but a significantly higher risk of pneumonia in those treated with ICS/LABA.[128]

> ## ▶ BRONCHODILATORS IN STABLE COPD

- Inhaled bronchodilators in COPD are central to symptom management and commonly given on a regular basis to prevent or reduce symptoms (**Evidence A**).
- Regular and as-needed use of SABA or SAMA improves FEV_1 and symptoms (**Evidence A**).
- Combinations of SABA and SAMA are superior compared to either medication alone in improving FEV_1 and symptoms (**Evidence A**).
- LABAs and LAMAs significantly improve lung function, dyspnea, health status, and reduce exacerbation rates (**Evidence A**).
- LAMAs have a greater effect on exacerbation reduction compared with LABAs (**Evidence A**) and decrease hospitalizations (**Evidence B**).
- Combination treatment with a LABA and LAMA increases FEV_1 and reduces symptoms compared to monotherapy (**Evidence A**).
- Combination treatment with a LABA/LAMA reduces exacerbations compared to monotherapy (**Evidence B**).
- Tiotropium improves the effectiveness of pulmonary rehabilitation in increasing exercise performance (**Evidence B**).
- Theophylline exerts a small bronchodilator effect in stable COPD (**Evidence A**) and that is associated with modest symptomatic benefits (**Evidence B**).

Anti-inflammatory agents

To date, exacerbations (e.g., exacerbation rate, patients with at least one exacerbation, time-to-first exacerbation) represent the main clinically relevant end-point used for efficacy assessment of drugs with anti-inflammatory effects (**see Table**).

Inhaled corticosteroids (ICS)

Preliminary general considerations. In vitro evidence suggests that COPD-associated inflammation has limited responsiveness to corticosteroids. Moreover, some drugs including beta$_2$-agonists, theophylline or macrolides may partially facilitate corticosteroid sensitivity in COPD.[129,130] The clinical relevance of this effect has not yet been fully established.

In vivo data suggest that the dose-response relationships and long-term (> 3 years) safety of inhaled corticosteroids (ICS) in patients with COPD are unclear and require further investigation.[109] Because the effects of ICS in COPD can be modulated by the concomitant use of long-acting bronchodilators, these two therapeutic options are discussed separately.

Efficacy of ICS (alone). Most studies have found that regular treatment with ICS alone does not modify the long-term decline of FEV_1 nor mortality in patients with COPD.[131] Studies and meta-analyses assessing the effect of regular treatment with ICS alone on mortality in patients with COPD have not provided conclusive evidence of benefit.[131] In the TORCH trial, a trend toward higher mortality was observed for patients treated with fluticasone propionate alone compared to those receiving placebo or salmeterol plus fluticasone propionate combination.[132] However, an increase in mortality was not observed in COPD patients treated with fluticasone furoate in the Survival in Chronic Obstructive Pulmonary Disease with Heightened Cardiovascular Risk (SUMMIT) trial.[133] However, in moderate COPD, fluticasone furoate alone or in combination with vilanterol was associated with slower decline in FEV_1 compared with placebo or vilanterol alone by on average 9 ml/year.[134]

▶ ANTI-INFLAMMATORY THERAPY IN STABLE COPD

INHALED CORTICOSTEROIDS

- An ICS combined with a LABA is more effective than the individual components in improving lung function and health status and reducing exacerbations in patients with exacerbations and moderate to very severe COPD **(Evidence A)**.

- Regular treatment with ICS increases the risk of pneumonia especially in those with severe disease **(Evidence A)**.

- Triple inhaled therapy of ICS/LAMA/LABA improves lung function, symptoms and health status and reduces exacerbations compared to ICS/LABA, LABA/LAMA or LAMA monotherapy **(Evidence A)**.

ORAL GLUCOCORTICOIDS

- Long-term use of oral glucocorticoids has numerous side effects **(Evidence A)** with no evidence of benefits **(Evidence C)**.

PDE4 INHIBITORS

- In patients with chronic bronchitis, severe to very severe COPD and a history of exacerbations:
  - » A PDE4 inhibitor improves lung function and reduces moderate and severe exacerbations **(Evidence A)**.
  - » A PDE4 inhibitor improves lung function and decreases exacerbations in patients who are on fixed-dose LABA/ICS combinations **(Evidence A)**.

ANTIBIOTICS

- Long-term azithromycin and erythromycin therapy reduces exacerbations over one year **(Evidence A)**.

- Treatment with azithromycin is associated with an increased incidence of bacterial resistance **(Evidence A)** and hearing test impairments **(Evidence B)**.

MUCOREGULATORS AND ANTIOXIDANT AGENTS

- Regular treatment with mucolytics such as erdosteine, carbocysteine and NAC reduces the risk of exacerbations in select populations **(Evidence B)**.

OTHER ANTI-INFLAMMATORY AGENTS

- Simvastatin does not prevent exacerbations in COPD patients at increased risk of exacerbations and without indications for statin therapy **(Evidence A)**. However, observational studies suggest that statins may have positive effects on some outcomes in patients with COPD who receive them for cardiovascular and metabolic indications **(Evidence C)**.

- Leukotriene modifiers have not been tested adequately in COPD patients.

ICS in combination with long-acting bronchodilator therapy. In patients with moderate to very severe COPD and exacerbations, an ICS combined with a LABA is more effective than either component alone in improving lung function, health status and reducing exacerbations.[135,136] Clinical trials powered on all-cause mortality as the primary outcome failed to demonstrate a statistically significant effect of combination therapy on survival.[132,133]

Most studies that found a beneficial effect of LABA/ICS fixed dose combination (FDC) over LABA alone on exacerbation rate, recruited patients with a history of at least one exacerbation in the previous year.[135] A pragmatic RCT conducted in a primary healthcare setting in the United Kingdom compared a LABA/ICS combination with usual care. Findings showed an 8.4% reduction in moderate-to-severe exacerbations (primary outcome) and a significant improvement in CAT™ score, with no difference in the rate of healthcare contacts or pneumonias. However, basing recommendations on these results is difficult because of the heterogeneity of treatments reported in the usual care group, the higher rate of treatment changes in the group receiving the LABA/ICS combination of interest, and the medical practice patterns unique to the UK region where the study was conducted.[137]

Blood eosinophil count. A number of recent studies have shown that blood eosinophil counts predict the magnitude of the effect of ICS (added on top of regular maintenance bronchodilator treatment) in preventing future exacerbations.[127,138-142] There is a continuous relationship between blood eosinophil counts and ICS effects; no and/or small effects are observed at lower eosinophil counts, with incrementally increasing effects observed at higher eosinophil counts. Data modelling indicates that ICS containing regimens have little or no effect at a blood eosinophil count < 100 cells/μL,[138] therefore this threshold can be used to identify patients with a low likelihood of treatment benefit with ICS. The threshold of a blood eosinophil count > 300 cells/μL identifies the top of the continuous relationship between eosinophils and ICS, and can be used to identify patients with the greatest likelihood of treatment benefit with ICS. These thresholds of < 100 cells/μL and > 300 cells/μL should be regarded as estimates, rather than precise cut-off values, that can predict different probabilities of treatment benefit. All in all, therefore, blood eosinophil counts can help clinicians estimate the likelihood of a beneficial preventive response to the addition of ICS to regular bronchodilator treatment, and thus can be used as a biomarker in conjunction with clinical assessment when making decisions regarding ICS use.

Sources of evidence include: 1) *Post-hoc* analyses comparing ICS/LABA versus LABA[138,139,141]; 2) Pre-specified analyses comparing triple therapy versus LAMA/LABA or LAMA[127,140,142] and, 3) other analyses comparing ICS/LABA versus LABA/LAMA[143] or studying ICS withdrawal.[144-146]

The treatment effect of ICS containing regimens (ICS/LAMA/LABA and ICS/LABA vs LABA/LAMA) is higher in patients with high exacerbation risk (≥ 2 exacerbations and / or 1 hospitalization in the previous year).[126,127,140] Thus, the use of blood eosinophil counts to predict ICS effects should always be combined with clinical assessment of exacerbation risk (as indicated by the previous history of exacerbations). Other factors (smoking status, ethnicity, geographical location) could influence the relationship between ICS effect and blood eosinophil count, but remains to be further explored. The mechanism for an increased ICS effect in COPD patients with higher blood eosinophil counts remains unclear.

The repeatability of blood eosinophil counts in a large primary care population appears reasonable,[147] although greater variability is observed at higher thresholds.[148] Better reproducibility is observed at the lower thresholds (e.g., 100 cells/μL).[149]

Cohort studies have produced differing results with regard to the ability of blood eosinophils to predict future exacerbation outcomes, with either no relationship[150] or a positive relationship reported.[151,152] Differences between studies are likely to be related to different previous exacerbation histories and ICS use. There is insufficient evidence to recommend that blood eosinophils should be used to predict future exacerbation risk on an individual basis in

COPD patients. Factors to consider when initiating ICS treatment in combination with one or two long-acting bronchodilators are shown in the **Figure**.[153]

Adverse effects. There is high quality evidence from randomized controlled trials (RCTs) that ICS use is associated with higher prevalence of oral candidiasis, hoarse voice, skin bruising and pneumonia.[131] This excess risk has been confirmed in ICS studies using fluticasone furoate, even at low doses.[154] Patients at higher risk of pneumonia include those who currently smoke, are aged ≥ 55 years, have a history of prior exacerbations or pneumonia, a body mass index (BMI) < 25 kg/m^2, a poor MRC dyspnea grade and/or severe airflow limitation.[155,156] Independent of ICS use, there is evidence that a blood eosinophil count < 2% increases the risk of developing pneumonia.[157] In studies of patients with moderate COPD, ICS by itself or in combination with a LABA did not increase the risk of pneumonia.[133,156]

Results from RCTs have yielded varied results regarding the risk of decreased bone density and fractures with ICS treatment, which may be due to differences in study designs and/or differences between ICS compounds.[72,154,158-160] Results of observational studies suggest that ICS treatment could also be associated with increased risk of diabetes/poor control of diabetes,[161] cataracts,[162] and mycobacterial infection[163] including tuberculosis.[164,165] In the absence of RCT data on these issues, it is not possible to draw firm conclusions.[166] An increased risk of tuberculosis has been found in both observational studies and a meta-analysis of RCTs.[124,125]

Withdrawal of ICS. Results from withdrawal studies provide equivocal results regarding consequences of withdrawal on lung function, symptoms and exacerbations.[167-171] Some studies, but not all, have shown an increase in exacerbations and/or symptoms following ICS withdrawal, while others have not. There has been evidence for a modest decrease in FEV$_1$ (approximately 40 mL) with ICS withdrawal,[171] which could be associated with increased baseline circulating eosinophil level.[144] A recent study examining ICS withdrawal on a background of dual bronchodilator therapy demonstrated that both FEV$_1$ loss and an increase in exacerbation frequency associated with ICS withdrawal was greatest among patients with a blood eosinophil count ≥ 300 cells/μl at baseline.[146] Differences between studies may relate to differences in methodology, including the use of background long-acting bronchodilator medication(s) which may minimize any effect of ICS withdrawal.

Triple inhaled therapy

The step up in inhaled treatment to LABA plus LAMA plus ICS (triple therapy) can occur by various approaches.[172] This may improve lung function, patient reported outcomes and prevent exacerbations.[173-176] Adding a LAMA to existing LABA/ICS improves lung function and patient reported outcomes, in particular exacerbation risk.[174,177-180] A double-blind, parallel group, RCT reported that treatment with single inhaler triple therapy had greater clinical benefits compared to tiotropium in patients with symptomatic COPD, $FEV_1 < 50\%$, and a history of exacerbations,[142] and double-blind RCTs have reported benefits of single-inhaler triple therapy compared with LABA/LAMA combination therapy.[127,140]

The search for a mortality benefit with inhaled respiratory medications in patients with COPD has been elusive. Prior large, prospective and randomized trials with mortality as the primary endpoint failed to show a statistically significant survival benefit with salmeterol/fluticasone propionate or vilanterol/fluticasone furoate compared to the mono-components and placebo.[132,133] Recently, trials utilizing triple combinations of LABA/LAMA/ICS in comparison to LAMA, LABA/LAMA or LABA/ICS have reported reduced mortality with triple therapy.[181] Unlike previous trials, the recent studies target patient populations that are enriched increased respiratory symptoms and a prior history of frequent and/or severe exacerbations with the majority receiving background treatment with triple or LABA/ICS based therapy before study enrollment. The largest of these trials (n=10,355) compared single inhaler triple therapy versus ICS/LABA or LABA/LAMA dual therapy[127]; there was a statistically significant 42.1% reduction in the risk of on-treatment all-cause mortality and a 28.6% reduction in the risk of all-cause mortality including off-treatment data, comparing triple therapy with LABA/LAMA.[183] Independently adjudicated findings reported reduced cardiovascular and respiratory deaths, and deaths associated with COPD. A *post-hoc* pooled analysis of triple therapy clinical trials conducted in severe COPD patients with a history of exacerbations showed a trend for lower mortality with use of triple inhaled therapy compared to non-ICS based treatments, but the differences were not statistically significant.[181] By contrast, smaller studies that have examined triple inhaled therapy for shorter durations in patients less severely obstructed without prior frequent or severe exacerbations have failed to show any mortality benefit.[182] It should be noted that none of the recent studies reporting a reduction in mortality with triple inhaled therapy had survival as the primary endpoint.[127,140,142]

These effects are most likely to be seen in patients with COPD who are severely symptomatic, have moderate to very severe airflow obstruction and a history of frequent and/or severe exacerbations. Additionally, if de-escalating ICS is considered after respiratory stability is achieved in this patient group, it should be done with caution.

Oral glucocorticoids

Oral glucocorticoids have numerous side effects, including steroid myopathy[184] which can contribute to muscle weakness, decreased functionality, and respiratory failure in subjects with very severe COPD. Systemic glucocorticoids for treating acute exacerbations in hospitalized patients, or during emergency department visits, have been shown to reduce the rate of treatment failure, the rate of relapse and improve lung function and breathlessness.[185] Conversely, prospective studies on the long-term effects of oral glucocorticoids in stable COPD are limited.[186,187] Therefore, while oral glucocorticoids play a role in the acute management of exacerbations, they have no role in the chronic daily treatment in COPD because of a lack of benefit balanced against a high rate of systemic complications.

Phosphodiesterase-4 (PDE4) inhibitors

Efficacy. The principal action of PDE4 inhibitors is to reduce inflammation by inhibiting the breakdown of intracellular cyclic AMP.[188] Roflumilast is a once daily oral medication with no direct bronchodilator activity. Roflumilast reduces moderate and severe exacerbations treated with systemic corticosteroids in patients with chronic bronchitis, severe to very severe COPD, and a history of exacerbations.[189] The effects on lung function are

21

also seen when roflumilast is added to long-acting bronchodilators,[190] and in patients who are not controlled on fixed-dose LABA/ICS combinations.[191] The beneficial effects of roflumilast have been reported to be greater in patients with a prior history of hospitalization for an acute exacerbation.[192,193] There has been no study directly comparing roflumilast with an inhaled corticosteroid.

Adverse effects. PDE4 inhibitors have more adverse effects than inhaled medications for COPD.[194] The most frequent are diarrhea, nausea, reduced appetite, weight loss, abdominal pain, sleep disturbance, and headache. Roflumilast should also be used with caution in patients with depression.

Antibiotics

- In older studies prophylactic, *continuous* use of antibiotics had no effect on the frequency of exacerbations in COPD[195,196] and a study that examined the efficacy of chemoprophylaxis undertaken in winter months over a period of 5 years concluded that there was no benefit.[197]
- More recent studies have shown that regular use of some antibiotics may reduce exacerbation rate.[198,199]
- Azithromycin (250 mg/day or 500 mg three times per week) or erythromycin (500 mg two times per day) for one year in patients prone to exacerbations reduced the risk of exacerbations compared to usual care.[200-202]

Adverse effects. Azithromycin use was associated with an increased incidence of bacterial resistance, prolongation of QTc interval, and impaired hearing tests.[202]

Mucolytic (mucokinetics, mucoregulators) and antioxidant agents (NAC, carbocysteine)

- In COPD patients not receiving inhaled corticosteroids, regular treatment with mucolytics such as erdosteine, carbocysteine and N-acetylcysteine may reduce exacerbations and modestly improve health status.[203-205]

Other drugs with anti-inflammatory potential

Two RCTs in COPD patients performed before 2005 that investigated the use of an immunoregulator reported a decrease in the severity and frequency of exacerbations.[206,207] Additional studies are needed to examine the long-term effects of this therapy in patients receiving currently recommended COPD maintenance therapy.

More recently four large phase 3 studies have investigated the efficacy of the anti-IL-5 monoclonal antibody mepolizumab[208] and the anti-IL-5 receptor-α antibody benralizumab[209] in patients with severe COPD, recurrent exacerbations and peripheral blood evidence of eosinophilic inflammation despite high intensity inhaled therapy. The studies showed a 15-20% reduction in the rate of severe exacerbations but the effect was not always statistically significant and it was variable between studies and doses. There was no effect on FEV_1 or quality of life scores and no consistent relationship between the response to treatment and the peripheral blood eosinophil count. A *post-hoc* analysis of the mepolizumab trial showed greater benefit and more clear evidence of a blood eosinophil related treatment effect against oral corticosteroid treated exacerbations raising the possibility that this treatment might find a role in a highly selected subgroup of patients with eosinophilic COPD and frequent requirement for oral corticosteroids. Further studies are required to investigate this possibility.

Nedocromil and leukotriene modifiers have not been tested adequately in COPD patients and the available evidence does not support their use. [210,211]

There was no evidence of benefit, and some evidence of harm, including malignancy and pneumonia, following treatment with an anti-TNF-alpha antibody (infliximab) in moderate to severe COPD.[212]

Simvastatin did not prevent exacerbations in patients with COPD who had no metabolic or cardiovascular indication for statin treatment.[213] An association between statin use and improved outcomes (including decreased exacerbations and mortality) has been reported in observational studies of patients with COPD who received them for cardiovascular and metabolic indications.[214]

There is no evidence that supplementation with vitamin D has a positive impact on exacerbations in unselected patients.[215] In a recent meta-analysis vitamin D supplementation reduced exacerbation rates in patients with low baseline vitamin D levels.[216]

Issues related to inhaled delivery

▶ THE INHALED ROUTE

- When a treatment is given by the inhaled route, the importance of education and training in inhaler device technique cannot be over-emphasized.

- The choice of inhaler device has to be individually tailored and will depend on access, cost, prescriber, and most importantly, patient's ability and preference.

- It is essential to provide instructions and to demonstrate the proper inhalation technique when prescribing a device, to ensure that inhaler technique is adequate and re-check at each visit that patients continue to use their inhaler correctly.

- Inhaler technique (and adherence to therapy) should be assessed before concluding that the current therapy is insufficient.

Other pharmacological treatments

▶ OTHER PHARMACOLOGICAL TREATMENTS

ALPHA-1 ANTITRYPSIN AUGMENTATION THERAPY
- Intravenous augmentation therapy may slow down the progression of emphysema (**Evidence B**).

ANTITUSSIVES
- There is no conclusive evidence of a beneficial role of antitussives in patients with COPD (**Evidence C**).

VASODILATORS
- Vasodilators do not improve outcomes and may worsen oxygenation (**Evidence B**).

REHABILITATION, EDUCATION & SELF-MANAGEMENT

Pulmonary rehabilitation

Pulmonary rehabilitation is defined as "a comprehensive intervention based on thorough patient assessment followed by patient-tailored therapies that include, but are not limited to, exercise training, education, self-management intervention aiming at behavior change, designed to improve the physical and psychological condition of people with chronic respiratory disease and to promote the long-term adherence to health-enhancing behaviors."[217] The benefits to COPD patients from pulmonary rehabilitation are considerable (**see Table**), and

23

rehabilitation has been shown to be the most effective therapeutic strategy to improve shortness of breath, health status and exercise tolerance.[218]

PULMONARY REHABILITATION, SELF-MANAGEMENT AND INTEGRATIVE CARE IN COPD

PULMONARY REHABILITATION

- Pulmonary rehabilitation improves dyspnea, health status and exercise tolerance in stable patients **(Evidence A)**.

- Pulmonary rehabilitation reduces hospitalization among patients who have had a recent exacerbation (≤4 weeks from prior hospitalization) **(Evidence B)**.

- Pulmonary rehabilitation leads to a reduction in symptoms of anxiety and depression **(Evidence A)**.

EDUCATION AND SELF-MANAGEMENT

- Education alone has not been shown to be effective **(Evidence C)**.

- Self-management intervention with communication with a health care professional improves health status and decreases hospitalizations and emergency department visits **(Evidence B)**.

INTEGRATED CARE PROGRAMS

- Integrative care and telehealth have no demonstrated benefit at this time **(Evidence B)**.

SUPPORTIVE, PALLIATIVE, END-OF-LIFE & HOSPICE CARE

Symptom control and palliative care

Palliative care is a broad term that encompasses approaches to symptom control as well as management of terminal patients close to death. The goal of palliative care is to prevent and relieve suffering, and to support the best possible quality of life for patients and their families, regardless of the stage of disease or the need for other therapies.[219] Even when receiving optimal medical therapy many patients with COPD continue to experience distressing breathlessness, impaired exercise capacity, fatigue, and suffer panic, anxiety and depression **(see Table)**.[220]

PALLIATIVE CARE, END OF LIFE AND HOSPICE CARE IN COPD

- Opiates, neuromuscular electrical stimulation (NMES), oxygen and fans blowing air on to the face can relieve breathlessness **(Evidence C)**.

- In malnourished patients, nutritional supplementation may improve respiratory muscle strength and overall health status **(Evidence B)**.

- Fatigue can be improved by self-management education, pulmonary rehabilitation, nutritional support and mind-body interventions **(Evidence B)**.

OTHER TREATMENTS

Oxygen therapy and ventilatory support

Oxygen therapy. The long-term administration of oxygen (> 15 hours per day) to patients with chronic respiratory failure has been shown to increase survival in patients with severe resting hypoxemia.[221] Breathlessness may be relieved in COPD patients who are either mildly hypoxemic, or non-hypoxemic but do not otherwise qualify for home oxygen therapy, when oxygen is given during exercise training; however, studies have shown no improvement of breathlessness in daily life and no benefit on health related quality of life **(see Table)**.[222,223]

> ## OXYGEN THERAPY AND VENTILATORY SUPPORT IN STABLE COPD

> **OXYGEN THERAPY**

> - The long-term administration of oxygen increases survival in patients with severe chronic resting arterial hypoxemia **(Evidence A)**.
>
> - In patients with stable COPD and moderate resting or exercise-induced arterial desaturation, prescription of long-term oxygen does not lengthen time to death or first hospitalization or provide sustained benefit in health status, lung function and 6-minute walk distance **(Evidence A)**.
>
> - Resting oxygenation at sea level does not exclude the development of severe hypoxemia when traveling by air **(Evidence C)**.

> **VENTILATORY SUPPORT**

> - NPPV may improve hospitalization-free survival in selected patients after recent hospitalization, particularly in those with pronounced daytime persistent hypercapnia ($PaCO_2 \geq 52$ mmHg) **(Evidence B)**.

Ventilatory Support

During exacerbations of COPD. Noninvasive ventilation (NIV) in the form of noninvasive positive pressure ventilation (NPPV) is the standard of care for decreasing morbidity and mortality in patients hospitalized with an exacerbation of COPD and acute respiratory failure.[224-226]

Stable patient. In patients with both COPD and obstructive sleep apnea there are clear benefits associated with the use of continuous positive airway pressure (CPAP) to improve both survival and the risk of hospital admissions.[227]

- Whether to use NPPV chronically at home to treat patients with acute on chronic respiratory failure following hospitalization remains undetermined and outcome may be affected by persistent hypercapnia.[228]
- A recent multicenter (13 sites) prospective RCT of COPD patients (n=116) with persistent hypercapnia ($PaCO_2$ >53 mmHg) showed that adding home NIV to oxygen therapy significantly prolonged the time to readmission or death within 12 months.[228]
- Two previous retrospective studies[229,230] and two of three RCTs[228,231-234] reported reductions in re-hospitalization and improved survival with using NPPV post-hospitalization.
- In patients with both COPD and obstructive sleep apnea there are clear benefits associated with the use of continuous positive airway pressure (CPAP) to improve both survival and the risk of hospital admissions.[227]

Surgical Interventions

Lung volume reduction surgery (LVRS). LVRS is a surgical procedure in which parts of the lungs are resected to reduce hyperinflation,[235] making respiratory muscles more effective pressure generators by improving their mechanical efficiency.[236,237] LVRS increases the elastic recoil pressure of the lung and thus improves expiratory flow rates and reduces exacerbations.[238,239]

Lung transplantation. In appropriately selected patients with very severe COPD, lung transplantation has been shown to improve health status and functional capacity but not prolong survival.[240-242] Over 70% of lung transplants conducted in COPD patients are double lung transplants; the remainder are single lung transplants.[243] Bilateral lung transplantation has been reported to provide longer survival than single lung transplantation in COPD patients, especially those < 60 years of age.[244] The median survival for lung transplantation in all COPD patients has increased to 5.5 years; it is 7 years in those receiving a bilateral lung transplant and 5 years in those receiving a single lung transplant.[243]

> ## ▶ INTERVENTIONAL THERAPY IN STABLE COPD

LUNG VOLUME REDUCTION SURGERY

- Lung volume reduction surgery improves survival in severe emphysema patients with an upper–lobe emphysema and low post–rehabilitation exercise capacity (**Evidence A**).

BULLECTOMY

- In selected patients, bullectomy is associated with decreased dyspnea, improved lung function and exercise tolerance (**Evidence C**).

TRANSPLANTATION

- In appropriately selected patients with very severe COPD, lung transplantation has been shown to improve quality of life and functional capacity (**Evidence C**).

BRONCHOSCOPIC INTERVENTIONS

- In select patients with advanced emphysema, bronchoscopic interventions reduce end-expiratory lung volume and improve exercise tolerance, health status and lung function at 6-12 months following treatment. Endobronchial valves (**Evidence A**); Lung coils (**Evidence B**); Vapor ablation (**Evidence B**).

Bronchoscopic interventions to reduce hyperinflation in severe emphysema

Due to the morbidity and mortality associated with LVRS, less invasive bronchoscopic approaches to lung reduction have been examined.[245] These include a variety of different bronchoscopic procedures.[245] Although these techniques differ markedly from one another they are similar in their objective to decrease thoracic volume to improve lung, chest wall and respiratory muscle mechanics.

Prospective studies have shown that the use of bronchial stents is not effective.[246] A multicenter study examining the effects of a lung sealant to create lung reduction was discontinued prematurely; while the study reported significant benefits in some physiologic parameters, the intervention was associated with significant morbidity and mortality.[247]

A large prospective multicenter RCT of endobronchial valve placement showed statistically significant improvements in FEV_1 and 6-minute walk distance compared to control therapy at 6 months post intervention.[248] However, the magnitude of the observed improvements was not clinically meaningful. Subsequently, efficacy of the same endobronchial valve has been studied in patients with heterogeneous,[249] or heterogeneous and homogenous emphysema[27] with mixed outcomes. Non-significant increases in median FEV_1 at three months post valve implantation in one study was attributed to valve placement in some patients with interlobar collateral ventilation.[249] Another study showed significant increases in FEV_1 and 6-minute walk distance in subjects selected for the absence of interlobar collateral ventilation compared to the control group at 6 months.[27] Adverse effects in the endobronchial valve treatment group in both studies included pneumothorax, valve removal or valve replacement.[27] Greater benefit was shown in patents with heterogeneous compared to those with homogenous emphysema.[27] An RCT of endobronchial valve placement compared with usual care conducted only in homogenous emphysematous patients without interlobar collateral ventilation reported improvements in FEV_1, 6-minute walk distance and health status at 6 months with targeted lobe reduction in 97% of subjects as measured by volumetric CT (mean reduction 1,195 ml).[250] A large multicenter, prospective, RCT of endobronchial valve treatment in patients with heterogeneous emphysema distribution and little to no collateral ventilation, demonstrated significant clinically meaningful benefits over current standard care in lung function, dyspnea, exercise capacity, and quality of life out to at least 12-months post-procedure.[251] Pneumothorax was seen in 26.6% of subjects treated with the endobronchial valve usually within the first 72 hours of the procedure (76%).[250-252] Another large multicenter prospective RCT using a different type of endobronchial valve in patients selected for targeted lobe treatment based on fissure integrity assessed by high resolution chest CT showed a significant between-group increase in mean FEV_1 from baseline (0.101L) and a 25.7% between-group difference in FEV_1 responder rates (improvement ≥15%). These results persisted at 12 months. The endobronchial valve treated group also had significant reductions in hyperinflation and dyspnea. Improved health status and quality of life was also observed. Consistent with prior studies, pneumothorax occurred in 25.5% of endobronchial valve treated patients; the majority occurred in the first three days following the procedure during the period of average hospitalization. Early-onset pneumothorax in the endobronchial valve treatment group likely results from lung conformation changes due to acute volume reduction in the emphysematous targeted lobe by valve therapy that triggers rapid ipsilateral non-targeted lobe expansion, a recognized indicator of successful target lobe occlusion in patients with intact fissures or absence of collateral ventilation.[253] The occurrence of pneumothorax highlights the need for physicians performing this procedure to have expertise in the management of procedural complications.[253] After the post-procedural period however, patients treated with the endobronchial valve compared to usual care tend to have a lower number of exacerbations and episodes of respiratory failure. A comparison of treatment benefits and complications associated with endobronchial valve placement compared to LVRS show comparable benefits with endobronchial valve treatment but with fewer complications.[251] Endobronchial valve therapy is now clinically available and approved for treatment in many countries in the treatment of patients who have intact fissures or lack of collateral ventilation.[251,254,255]

Other bronchoscopic lung volume reduction techniques do not depend upon the presence of intact fissures or absence of collateral ventilation. In a prospective RCT, targeted thermal vapour ablation of more diseased segments resulted in clinically meaningful and statistically significant improvements in lung function and health status at 6 months. COPD exacerbation was the most common serious adverse event. Durability of these changes was subsequently reported at 12 months follow-up.[256,257] This therapy has limited clinical availability.

Two multicenter trials have examined nitinol coils implanted into the lung compared to usual care on changes in 6-minute walk distance, lung function and health status in patients with advanced homogenous and heterogeneous emphysema. Both studies reported an increase in 6-minute walk distance with coil treatment compared to control and smaller improvements in FEV_1, and quality of life measured by St George's Respiratory Questionnaire.[258,259] Major complications included pneumonia, pneumothorax, hemoptysis and COPD exacerbations occurring more frequently in the coil group.[259] This therapy has limited clinical availability.

Additional data are needed to define the optimal bronchoscopic lung volume technique to produce bronchoscopic lung volume reduction in patients who lack fissure integrity, or exhibit collateral ventilation, and to refine the procedure to reduce complications and improve longer term clinical outcomes.[259]

MANAGEMENT OF STABLE COPD

OVERALL KEY POINTS:

- *The management strategy for stable COPD should be predominantly based on the individualized assessment of symptoms and future risk of exacerbations.*

- *All individuals who smoke should be strongly encouraged and supported to quit.*

- *The main treatment goals are reduction of symptoms and future risk of exacerbations.*

- *Management strategies include pharmacologic and non-pharmacologic interventions.*

COPD patients should have an assessment of the severity of their airflow obstruction, symptoms, history of exacerbations, exposure to risk factors and comorbidities (**Figure**) to guide management. The assessment is summarized in **Chapter 2**.

We propose a tailored approach to initiate treatment based on the level of symptoms and risk for exacerbations. Treatment can be escalated/de-escalated based on the presence of the predominant symptoms of breathlessness and exercise limitation, and the continued occurrence of exacerbations whilst on maintenance therapy. The basis for these recommendations, which propose an organized approach to treatment, was partly derived from evidence generated from randomized controlled trials. However, as these recommendations are intended to support clinician decision-making, they also incorporate expert advice based on clinical experience.

It is crucial for people with COPD to understand the nature of the disease, risk factors for its progression, and the role that they and their healthcare workers must play in order to achieve optimal management and health outcomes.

Following the assessment, initial management should address reducing exposure to risk factors including smoking cessation. Vaccination should be offered, and patients should receive general advice on healthy living, including diet, and that physical exercise is safe and encouraged for people with COPD. Initial pharmacotherapy should be based on the patient's GOLD group (**Figure**). Patients should be offered guidance on self-management of breathlessness, energy conservation and stress management, and they should be given a written action plan. Comorbidities should also be managed (**Figure**).

Patients should be reviewed after a suitable interval and their current level of symptoms (using either the CAT or mMRC scores) and exacerbation frequency assessed. The effect of treatment and possible adverse effects should be evaluated, and comorbidities reassessed.

Inhaler technique; adherence to prescribed therapy (both pharmacological and non-pharmacological); smoking status and continued exposure to risk factors should be checked. Physical activity should be encouraged and referral for pulmonary rehabilitation considered. The need for oxygen therapy, ventilatory support, lung volume reduction and palliative approaches should be reviewed. The action plan should be updated. Spirometry should be repeated at least annually.

Pharmacological and non-pharmacological therapy should be adjusted as necessary (see below) and further reviews undertaken (**Figure**).

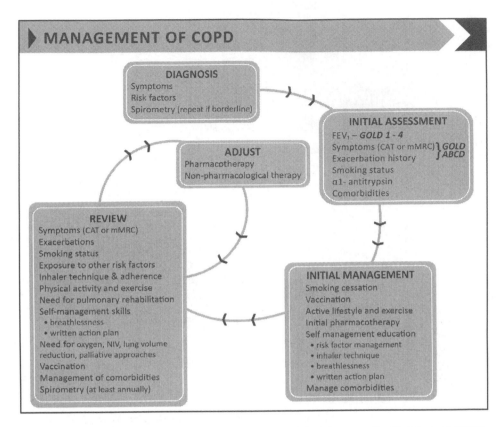

MANAGEMENT OF COPD

DIAGNOSIS
Symptoms
Risk factors
Spirometry (repeat if borderline)

INITIAL ASSESSMENT
FEV₁ – *GOLD 1 - 4*
Symptoms (CAT or mMRC) } *GOLD*
Exacerbation history } *ABCD*
Smoking status
α1- antitrypsin
Comorbidities

ADJUST
Pharmacotherapy
Non-pharmacological therapy

REVIEW
Symptoms (CAT or mMRC)
Exacerbations
Smoking status
Exposure to other risk factors
Inhaler technique & adherence
Physical activity and exercise
Need for pulmonary rehabilitation
Self-management skills
• breathlessness
• written action plan
Need for oxygen, NIV, lung volume
reduction, palliative approaches
Vaccination
Management of comorbidities
Spirometry (at least annually)

INITIAL MANAGEMENT
Smoking cessation
Vaccination
Active lifestyle and exercise
Initial pharmacotherapy
Self management education
• risk factor management
• inhaler technique
• breathlessness
• written action plan
Manage comorbidities

The goals for treatment of stable COPD are to improve symptoms, exercise tolerance and health status in addition to reducing risk by preventing disease progression, exacerbations and mortality.

IDENTIFY AND REDUCE EXPOSURE TO RISK FACTORS

Identification and reduction of exposure to risk factors (**see Tables**)[60,337,338] is important in the treatment and prevention of COPD. Cigarette smoking is the most commonly encountered and easily identifiable risk factor for COPD, and smoking cessation should be continually encouraged for all individuals who smoke. Reduction of total personal exposure to occupational dusts, fumes, and gases, and to indoor and outdoor air pollutants, should also be addressed.

- Smoking cessation interventions should be actively pursued in all COPD patients **(Evidence A)**.

- Efficient ventilation, non-polluting cooking stoves and similar interventions should be recommended **(Evidence B)**.

- Clinicians should advise patients to avoid continued exposures to potential irritants, if possible **(Evidence D)**.

▶ **TREATING TOBACCO USE AND DEPENDENCE:**
A CLINICAL PRACTICE GUIDELINE — MAJOR FINDINGS & RECOMMENDATIONS

- Tobacco dependence is a chronic condition that warrants repeated treatment until long-term or permanent abstinence is achieved.

- Effective treatments for tobacco dependence exist and all tobacco users should be offered these treatments.

- Clinicians and health care delivery systems must operationalize the consistent identification, documentation, and treatment of every tobacco user at every visit.

- Brief smoking cessation counseling is effective and every tobacco user should be offered such advice at every contact with health care providers.

- There is a strong dose-response relation between the intensity of tobacco dependence counseling and its effectiveness.

- Three types of counseling have been found to be especially effective: practical counseling, social support of family and friends as part of treatment, and social support arranged outside of treatment.

- First-line pharmacotherapies for tobacco dependence — varenicline, bupropion sustained release, nicotine gum, nicotine inhaler, nicotine nasal spray, and nicotine patch—are effective and at least one of these medications should be prescribed in the absence of contraindications.

- Financial incentive programs for smoking cessation may facilitate smoking cessation.

- Tobacco dependence treatments are cost effective interventions.

TREATMENT OF STABLE COPD: PHARMACOLOGICAL TREATMENT

Pharmacological therapies can reduce symptoms, and the risk and severity of exacerbations, as well as improve the health status and exercise tolerance of patients with COPD. Most of the drugs are inhaled so proper inhaler technique is highly relevant. Key points for the inhalation of drugs, bronchodilator use, the use of anti-inflammatory agents and the use of pharmacological treatments are summarized in the **Tables**.

▶ KEY POINTS FOR INHALATION OF DRUGS

- The choice of inhaler device has to be individually tailored and will depend on access, cost, prescriber, and most importantly, patient's ability and preference.

- It is essential to provide instructions and to demonstrate the proper inhalation technique when prescribing a device, to ensure that inhaler technique is adequate and re-check at each visit that patients continue to use their inhaler correctly.

- Inhaler technique (and adherence to therapy) should be assessed before concluding that the current therapy requires modification.

▶ KEY POINTS FOR THE USE OF BRONCHODILATORS

- LABAs and LAMAs are preferred over short-acting agents except for patients with only occasional dyspnea **(Evidence A)**, and for immediate relief of symptoms in patients already on long-acting bronchodilators for maintenance therapy.

- Patients may be started on single long-acting bronchodilator therapy or dual long-acting bronchodilator therapy. In patients with persistent dyspnea on one bronchodilator treatment should be escalated to two **(Evidence A)**.

- Inhaled bronchodilators are recommended over oral bronchodilators **(Evidence A)**.

- Theophylline is not recommended unless other long-term treatment bronchodilators are unavailable or unaffordable **(Evidence B)**.

▶ KEY POINTS FOR THE USE OF ANTI-INFLAMMATORY AGENTS

- Long-term monotherapy with ICS is not recommended **(Evidence A)**.

- Long-term treatment with ICS may be considered in association with LABAs for patients with a history of exacerbations despite appropriate treatment with long-acting bronchodilators **(Evidence A)**.

- Long-term therapy with oral corticosteroids is not recommended **(Evidence A)**.

- In patients with severe to very severe airflow limitation, chronic bronchitis and exacerbations the addition of a PDE4 inhibitor to a treatment with long acting bronchodilators with/without ICS can be considered **(Evidence B)**.

- Preferentially, but not only in former smokers with exacerbations despite appropriate therapy, macrolides, in particular azithromycin, can be considered **(Evidence B)**.

- Statin therapy is not recommended for prevention of exacerbations **(Evidence A)**.

- Antioxidant mucolytics are recommended only in selected patients **(Evidence A)**.

Algorithms for the assessment, initiation and follow-up management of pharmacological treatment

A model for the **INITIATION** of pharmacological management of COPD according to the individualized assessment of symptoms and exacerbation risk following the ABCD assessment scheme is shown. There is a lack of high-quality evidence supporting initial pharmacological treatment strategies in newly diagnosed COPD patients. **The Figure below** is an attempt to provide clinical guidance using the best available evidence.

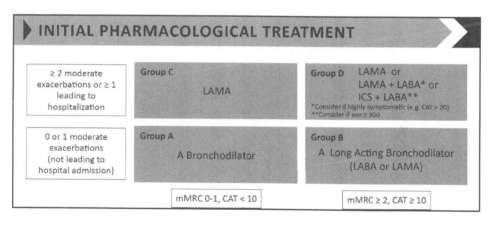

Definition of abbreviations: eos: blood eosinophil count in cells per microliter; mMRC: modified Medical Research Council dyspnea questionnaire; CAT™: COPD Assessment Test™.

Following implementation of therapy, patients should be reassessed for attainment of treatment goals and identification of any barriers for successful treatment. Following review of the patient response to treatment initiation, adjustments in pharmacological treatment may be needed.

A separate algorithm is provided for **FOLLOW-UP** treatment, where the management is still based on symptoms and exacerbations, but the recommendations do not depend on the patient's GOLD group at diagnosis (**see next Figure**). These follow-up recommendations are designed to facilitate management of patients taking maintenance treatment(s), whether early after initial treatment or after years of follow-up. These recommendations incorporate recent evidence from clinical trials and the use of peripheral blood eosinophil counts as a biomarker to guide the use of ICS therapy for exacerbation prevention.

32

1. **IF RESPONSE TO INITIAL TREATMENT IS APPROPRIATE, MAINTAIN IT.**
2. **IF NOT:**   ✓ Consider the predominant treatable trait to target (dyspnea or exacerbations)
   - Use exacerbation pathway if both exacerbations and dyspnea need to be targeted
   ✓ Place patient in box corresponding to current treatment & follow indications
   ✓ Assess response, adjust and review
   ✓ These recommendations do not depend on the ABCD assessment at diagnosis

• DYSPNEA •

LABA or LAMA

LABA + LAMA   ←** **   LABA + ICS

• Consider switching inhaler device or molecules
• Investigate (and treat) other causes of dyspnea   ←   LABA+LAMA+ICS

• EXACERBATIONS •

LABA or LAMA   *

LABA + LAMA   ←** **   LABA + ICS

Consider if eos < 100 | Consider if eos ≥100

LABA + LAMA+ ICS

Roflumilast
FEV$_1$ < 50% & chronic bronchitis

In former smokers
Azithromycin

eos = blood eosinophil count (cells/µL)
* Consider if eos ≥ 300 or eos ≥ 100 AND ≥2 moderate exacerbations / 1 hospitalization
** Consider de-escalation of ICS or switch if pneumonia, inappropriate original indication or lack of response to ICS

The **Figure above** suggests escalation and de-escalation strategies based on available efficacy as well as safety data. The response to treatment escalation should always be reviewed, and de-escalation should be considered if there is a lack of clinical benefit and/or side effects occur. De-escalation may also be considered in COPD patients receiving treatment who return with resolution of some symptoms that subsequently may require less therapy. Patients, in whom treatment modification is considered, in particular de-escalation, should be undertaken under close medical supervision. We are fully aware that treatment escalation has not been systematically tested; trials of de-escalation are also limited and only include ICS.

Initial pharmacological management
Rescue short-acting bronchodilators should be prescribed to all patients for immediate symptom relief.

Group A
▶ All Group A patients should be offered bronchodilator treatment based on its effect on breathlessness. This can be either a short- or a long-acting bronchodilator.

▶ This should be continued if benefit is documented.

<u>Group B</u>

▶ Initial therapy should consist of a long acting bronchodilator. Long-acting inhaled bronchodilators are superior to short-acting bronchodilators taken as needed i.e., *pro re nata* (prn) and are therefore recommended.[260,261]

▶ There is no evidence to recommend one class of long-acting bronchodilators over another for initial relief of symptoms in this group of patients. In the individual patient, the choice should depend on the patient's perception of symptom relief.

▶ For patients with severe breathlessness initial therapy with two bronchodilators may be considered.[121]

▶ Group B patients are likely to have comorbidities that may add to their symptomatology and impact their prognosis, and these possibilities should be investigated.[262,263]

<u>Group C</u>

▶ Initial therapy should consist of a single long acting bronchodilator. In two head-to-head comparisons[99,264] the tested LAMA was superior to the LABA regarding exacerbation prevention (for details see **Chapter 3**) therefore we recommend starting therapy with a LAMA in this group.

<u>Group D</u>

▶ In general, therapy can be started with a LAMA as it has effects on both breathlessness and exacerbations (see **Chapter 3**).

▶ For patients with more severe symptoms (order of magnitude of CAT™ ≥ 20), especially driven by greater dyspnea and / or exercise limitation, LAMA/LABA may be chosen as initial treatment based on studies with patient reported outcomes as the primary endpoint where LABA/LAMA combinations showed superior results compared to the single substances (see **Chapter 3**). An advantage of LABA/LAMA over LAMA for exacerbation prevention has not been consistently demonstrated, so the decision to use LABA/LAMA as initial treatment should be guided by the level of symptoms.

▶ In some patients, initial therapy with LABA/ICS may be the first choice; this treatment has the greatest likelihood of reducing exacerbations in patients with blood eosinophil counts ≥ 300 cells/μL. LABA/ICS may also be first choice in COPD patients with a history of asthma.

▶ ICS may cause side effects such as pneumonia,[155,264] so should be used as initial therapy only after the possible clinical benefits versus risks have been considered.

Follow-up pharmacological management

The follow-up pharmacological treatment algorithm can be applied to any patient who is already taking maintenance treatment(s) irrespective of the GOLD group allocated at treatment initiation. The need to treat primarily dyspnea/exercise limitation or prevent exacerbations further should be evaluated. If a change in treatment is considered necessary then select the corresponding algorithm for dyspnea or exacerbations; the exacerbation algorithm should also be used for patients who require a change in treatment for both dyspnea and exacerbations. Identify which box corresponds to the patient's the current treatment.

Follow up pharmacological management should be guided by the principles of first *review* and *assess*, then *adjust* if needed:

- ▷ Review
  - Review symptoms (dyspnea) and exacerbation risk.
- ▷ Assess
  - Assess inhaler technique and adherence, and the role of non-pharmacological approaches (covered later in this chapter).
- ▷ Adjust
  - Adjust pharmacological treatment, including escalation or de-escalation. Switching inhaler device or molecules within the same class (e.g. using a different long acting bronchodilator) may be considered as appropriate. Any change in treatment requires a subsequent *review* of the clinical response, including side effects.

Dyspnea

▷ For patients with persistent breathlessness or exercise limitation on ***long acting bronchodilator*** monotherapy,[265] the use of two bronchodilators is recommended.

- If the addition of a second long acting bronchodilator does not improve symptoms, we suggest the treatment could be stepped down again to monotherapy. Switching inhaler device or molecules can also be considered.

▷ For patients with persistent breathlessness or exercise limitation on ***LABA/ICS*** treatment, LAMA can be added to escalate to triple therapy.

- Alternatively, switching from LABA/ICS to LABA/LAMA should be considered if the original indication for ICS was inappropriate (e.g., an ICS was used to treat symptoms in the absence of a history of exacerbations), or there has been a lack of response to ICS treatment, or if ICS side effects warrant discontinuation.

▷ At all stages, dyspnea due to other causes (not COPD) should be investigated and treated appropriately. Inhaler technique and adherence should be considered as causes of inadequate treatment response.

Exacerbations

▷ For patients with persistent exacerbations on ***long acting bronchodilator*** monotherapy, escalation to either LABA/LAMA or LABA/ICS is recommended. LABA/ICS may be preferred for patients with a history or findings suggestive of asthma. Blood eosinophil counts may identify patients with a greater likelihood of a beneficial response to ICS. For patients with one exacerbation per year, a peripheral blood level ≥ 300 eosinophils/µL identifies patients more likely to respond to LABA/ICS treatment.[138,139] For patients with ≥ 2 moderate exacerbations per year or at least one severe exacerbation requiring hospitalization in the prior year, LABA/ICS treatment can be considered at blood eosinophil counts ≥ 100 cells/µL, as ICS effects are more pronounced in patients with greater exacerbation frequency and/or severity.[127]

▷ In patients who develop further exacerbations on **LABA/LAMA** therapy we suggest two alternative pathways. Blood eosinophil counts < 100 cells/µL can be used to predict a low likelihood of a beneficial ICS response:
- Escalation to LABA/LAMA/ICS. A beneficial response after the addition of ICS may be observed at blood eosinophil counts ≥ 100 cells /µL, with a greater magnitude of response more likely with higher eosinophil counts.

- Add roflumilast or azithromycin (see below) if blood eosinophils < 100 cells/µL.

▷ In patients who develop further exacerbations on **LABA/ICS** therapy, we recommend escalation to triple therapy by adding a LAMA.[127,179] Alternatively, treatment can be switched to LABA/LAMA if there has been a lack of response to ICS treatment, or if ICS side effects warrant discontinuation.

- If patients treated with **LABA/LAMA/ICS** who still have exacerbations the following options may be considered:
  - **Add roflumilast.** This may be considered in patients with an FEV_1 < 50% predicted and chronic bronchitis,[191] particularly if they have experienced at least one hospitalization for an exacerbation in the previous year.[192,266]
  - **Add a macrolide.** The best available evidence exists for the use of azithromycin, especially in those who are not current smokers.[193,202] Consideration to the development of resistant organisms should be factored into decision-making.
  - **Stopping ICS.** This can be considered if there are adverse effects (such as pneumonia) or a reported lack of efficacy. However, a blood eosinophil count ≥ 300 cells /μL identifies patients with the greatest likelihood of experiencing more exacerbations after ICS withdrawal and who subsequently should be followed closely for relapse of exacerbations.[145,146]

TREATMENT OF STABLE COPD: NON-PHARMACOLOGICAL TREATMENT

Non-pharmacological treatment is complementary to pharmacological treatment and should form part of the comprehensive management of COPD.

After receiving a diagnosis of COPD a patient should be given further information about the condition. Physicians should emphasize the importance of a smoke free environment, prescribe vaccinations, empower adherence to prescribed medication, ensure proper inhaler technique, promote physical activity and refer patients (GOLD B - GOLD D) to pulmonary rehabilitation.

Some relevant non-pharmacological measures based on the GOLD group **AT DIAGNOSIS** are summarized in the **Table** below.

▶ NON-PHARMACOLOGIC MANAGEMENT OF COPD*

PATIENT GROUP	ESSENTIAL	RECOMMENDED	DEPENDING ON LOCAL GUIDELINES
A	Smoking Cessation (can include pharmacologic treatment)	Physical Activity	Flu Vaccination
			Pneumococcal Vaccination
B, C and D	Smoking Cessation (can include pharmacologic treatment)	Physical Activity	Flu Vaccination
			Pneumococcal Vaccination
	Pulmonary Rehabilitation		

*Can include pharmacologic treatment.

Education and self-management

Self-management education and coaching by healthcare professionals should be a major component of the "Chronic Care Model" within the context of the healthcare delivery system.

The aim of self-management interventions is to motivate, engage and coach patients to positively adapt their health behavior(s) and develop skills to better manage their COPD on a day-to-day basis.[267] Physicians and healthcare providers need to go beyond pure education/advice-giving (didactic) approaches to help patients learn and adopt sustainable self-management skills. The basis of enabling patients to become active partners in their ongoing care is to build knowledge and skills. It is important to recognize that patient education alone does not itself change behavior or even motivate patients, and it has had no impact on improving exercise performance or lung function,[268,269] but it can play a role in improving skills, ability to cope with illness, and health status.[217]

▶ FOLLOW-UP OF NON-PHARMACOLOGICAL TREATMENT ⟩⟩

1. IF RESPONSE TO INITIAL TREATMENT IS APPROPRIATE, MAINTAIN IT AND OFFER:
- Flu vaccination every year and other recommended vaccinations according to guidelines
- Self-management education
- Assessment of behavioral risk factors such as smoking cessation (if applicable) and environmental exposures

Ensure
- Maintenance of exercise program and physical activity
- Adequate sleep and a healthy diet

2. IF NOT, CONSIDER THE PREDOMINANT TREATABLE TRAIT TO TARGET

• DYSPNEA •	• EXACERBATIONS •
▶ Self-management education (written action plan) with integrated self-management regarding:	▶ Self-management education (written action plan) that is personalized with respect to:
• Breathlessness and energy conservation techniques, and stress management strategies	• Avoidance of aggravating factors
▶ Pulmonary rehabilitation (PR) program and/or maintenance exercise program post PR	• How to monitor/manage worsening of symptoms
	• Contact information in the event of an exacerbation

All patients with advanced COPD should be considered for end of life and palliative care support to optimize symptom control and allow patients and their families to make informed choices about future management

TABLE 4.9

Oxygen therapy

An appropriate algorithm for the prescription of oxygen to COPD patients is shown below.

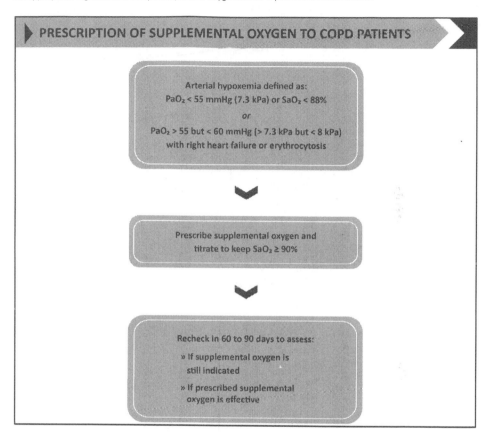

PRESCRIPTION OF SUPPLEMENTAL OXYGEN TO COPD PATIENTS

Arterial hypoxemia defined as:
$PaO_2 < 55$ mmHg (7.3 kPa) or $SaO_2 < 88\%$

or

$PaO_2 > 55$ but < 60 mmHg (> 7.3 kPa but < 8 kPa)
with right heart failure or erythrocytosis

Prescribe supplemental oxygen and
titrate to keep $SaO_2 \geq 90\%$

Recheck in 60 to 90 days to assess:

» If supplemental oxygen is
still indicated

» If prescribed supplemental
oxygen is effective

Key points for the use of non-pharmacological treatments are given in the following **Table**.

KEY POINTS FOR THE USE OF NON-PHARMACOLOGICAL TREATMENTS

EDUCATION, SELF-MANAGEMENT AND PULMONARY REHABILITATION

- Education is needed to change patient's knowledge but there is no evidence that used alone it will change patient behavior .
- Education self-management with the support of a case manager with or without the use of a written action plan is recommended for the prevention of exacerbation complications such as hospital admissions **(Evidence B)**.
- Rehabilitation is indicated in all patients with relevant symptoms and/or a high risk for exacerbation **(Evidence A)**.
- Physical activity is a strong predictor of mortality **(Evidence A)**. Patients should be encouraged to increase the level of physical activity although we still don't know how to best insure the likelihood of success.

VACCINATION

- Influenza vaccination is recommended for all patients with COPD **(Evidence A)**.
- Pneumococcal vaccination: the PCV13 and PPSV23 are recommended for all patients> 65 years of age, and in younger patients with significant comorbid conditions including chronic heart or lung disease **(Evidence B)**.

NUTRITION

- Nutritional supplementation should be considered in malnourished patients with COPD **(Evidence B)**.

END OF LIFE AND PALLIATIVE CARE

- All clinicians managing patients with COPD should be aware of the effectiveness of palliative approaches to symptom control and use these in their practice **(Evidence D)**.
- End of life care should include discussions with patients and their families about their views on resuscitation, advance directives and place of death preferences **(Evidence D)**.

TREATMENT OF HYPOXEMIA

- In patients with severe resting hypoxemia long-term oxygen therapy is indicated **(Evidence A)**.
- In patients with stable COPD and resting or exercise-induced moderate desaturation, long term oxygen treatment should not be routinely prescribed. However, individual patient factors may be considered when evaluating the patient's needs for supplemental oxygen **(Evidence A)**.
- Resting oxygenation at sea level does not exclude the development of severe hypoxemia when travelling by air **(Evidence C)**.

TREATMENT OF HYPERCAPNIA

- In patients with severe chronic hypercapnia and a history of hospitalization for acute respiratory failure, long term noninvasive ventilation may be considered **(Evidence B)**.

INTERVENTION BRONCHOSCOPY AND SURGERY

- Lung volume reduction surgery should be considered in selected patients with upper-lobe emphysema **(Evidence A)**.
- In selected patients with a large bulla surgical bullectomy may be considered **(Evidence C)**.
- In select patients with advanced emphysema, bronchoscopic interventions reduce end-expiratory lung volume and improve exercise tolerance, quality of life and lung function at 6-12 months following treatment. Endobronchial valves **(Evidence A)**; Lung coils **(Evidence B)**; Vapor ablation **(Evidence B)**.
- In patients with very severe COPD (progressive disease, BODE score of 7 to 10, and not candidate for lung volume reduction) lung transplantation may be considered for referral with at least one of the following: (1) history of hospitalization for exacerbation associated with acute hypercapnia (Pco_2 >50 mm Hg); (2) pulmonary hypertension and/or cor pulmonale, despite oxygen therapy; or (3) FEV_1 < 20% and either DLCO < 20% or homogenous distribution of emphysema **(Evidence C)**.

MONITORING AND FOLLOW-UP

Routine follow-up of COPD patients is essential. Lung function may worsen over time, even with the best available care. Symptoms, exacerbations and objective measures of airflow limitation should be monitored to determine when to modify management and to identify any complications and/or comorbidities that may develop. Based on current literature, comprehensive self-management or routine monitoring has not shown long-term benefits in terms of health status over usual care alone for COPD patients in general practice.[270]

MANAGEMENT OF EXACERBATIONS

OVERALL KEY POINTS:

- *An exacerbation of COPD is defined as an acute worsening of respiratory symptoms that results in additional therapy.*

- *As the symptoms are not specific to COPD relevant differential diagnoses should be considered.*

- *Exacerbations of COPD can be precipitated by several factors. The most common causes are respiratory tract infections.*

- *The goal for treatment of COPD exacerbations is to minimize the negative impact of the current exacerbation and to prevent subsequent events.*

- *Short-acting inhaled beta$_2$-agonists, with or without short-acting anticholinergics, are recommended as the initial bronchodilators to treat an acute exacerbation.*

- *Maintenance therapy with long-acting bronchodilators should be initiated as soon as possible before hospital discharge.*

- *Systemic corticosteroids can improve lung function (FEV$_1$), oxygenation and shorten recovery time and hospitalization duration. Duration of therapy should not be more than 5-7 days.*

- *Antibiotics, when indicated, can shorten recovery time, reduce the risk of early relapse, treatment failure, and hospitalization duration. Duration of therapy should be 5-7 days.*

- *Methylxanthines are not recommended due to increased side effect profiles.*

- *Non-invasive mechanical ventilation should be the first mode of ventilation used in COPD patients with acute respiratory failure who have no absolute contraindication because it improves gas exchange, reduces work of breathing and the need for intubation, decreases hospitalization duration and improves survival.*

- *Following an exacerbation, appropriate measures for exacerbation prevention should be initiated.*

An exacerbation of chronic obstructive pulmonary disease (COPD) is defined as an acute worsening of respiratory symptoms that results in additional therapy. [271,272] Exacerbations of COPD are important events in the management of COPD because they negatively impact health status, rates of hospitalization and readmission, and disease progression. COPD exacerbations are complex events usually associated with increased airway inflammation, increased mucus production and marked gas trapping. These changes contribute to increased dyspnea that is the key symptom of an exacerbation. Other symptoms include increased sputum purulence and volume, together with increased cough and wheeze.[273] As other comorbidities that may worsen respiratory symptoms are common in COPD patients, clinical assessment to rule out differential diagnoses should be considered before diagnosis of a COPD exacerbation (**Table**).

DIFFERENTIAL DIAGNOSIS OF COPD EXACERBATION

WHEN THERE IS CLINICAL SUSPICION OF THE FOLLOWING ACUTE CONDITIONS, CONSIDER THE FOLLOWING INVESTIGATIONS:

▶ **PNEUMONIA**
  - Chest radiograph
  - Assessment of C-reactive protein (CRP) and/or procalcitonin

▶ **PNEUMOTHORAX**
  - Chest radiograph or ultrasound

▶ **PLEURAL EFFUSION**
  - Chest radiograph or ultrasound

▶ **PULMONARY EMBOLISM**
  - D-dimer and/or Doppler sonogram of lower extremities
  - Chest tomography – pulmonary embolism protocol

▶ **PULMONARY EDEMA DUE TO CARDIAC RELATED CONDITIONS**
  - Electrocardiogram and cardiac ultrasound
  - Cardiac enzymes

▶ **CARDIAC ARRHYTHMIAS – ATRIAL FIBRILLATION/FLUTTER**
  - Electrocardiogram

Exacerbations are classified as:

- ▷ Mild (treated with short acting bronchodilators only, SABDs)
- ▷ Moderate (treated with SABDs plus antibiotics and/or oral corticosteroids) or
- ▷ Severe (patient requires hospitalization or visits the emergency room). Severe exacerbations may also be associated with acute respiratory failure.

It is now recognized that many exacerbations are not reported to healthcare professionals for therapy and yet these events, although often shorter in duration, also have a significant impact on health status.[274,275] Thus COPD patients need to receive education about the importance of understanding exacerbation symptoms and when to seek professional healthcare.

Exacerbations are mainly triggered by respiratory viral infections although bacterial infections and environmental factors such as pollution and ambient temperature may also initiate and/or amplify these events.[276] Short-term exposure to fine particulate matter (PM2.5) is associated with increased hospitalizations for acute exacerbations and increased mortality of COPD.[277-279] The most common virus isolated is human rhinovirus (the cause of the common cold) and can be detected for up to a week after an exacerbation onset.[276,280] When associated with viral infections, exacerbations are often more severe, last longer and precipitate more hospitalizations, as seen during winter.

Exacerbations can be associated with increased sputum production and, if purulent, there are studies that demonstrated increased bacteria in the sputum[273,280,281] There is reasonable evidence to support the concept that eosinophils are increased in the airways, lung, and blood in a significant proportion of patients with COPD. Furthermore, eosinophil numbers increase together with neutrophils and other inflammatory cells during exacerbations in a proportion of subjects with COPD exacerbations.[282-284] The presence of sputum eosinophilia has been related to susceptibility to viral infection.[281] It has been suggested that exacerbations associated with an increase in sputum or blood eosinophils may be more responsive to systemic steroids[285] although more prospective trials are needed to test this hypothesis.[285]

During a COPD exacerbation, symptoms usually last between 7 to 10 days, but some events may last longer. At 8 weeks, 20% of patients have not recovered to their pre-exacerbation state.[286] It is well established that COPD exacerbations contribute to disease progression.[287] Disease progression is even more likely if recovery from exacerbations is slow.[288] Exacerbations can also cluster in time and once a COPD patient experiences an exacerbation, they will show increased susceptibility to another event[289,290] (see **Chapter 2** of full report).

Some COPD patients are particularly susceptible to frequent exacerbations (defined as two or more exacerbations per year), and these patients have been shown to have worse health status and morbidity than patients with less frequent exacerbations.[272] Patients at high risk of frequent exacerbations can be recognized across all disease severity groups. The exact reason for an individual's increased susceptibility to exacerbation symptoms remains largely unknown. However, the perception of breathlessness is greater in frequent exacerbators than infrequent exacerbators,[291] suggesting that a perception of breathing difficulty may contribute to precipitating the respiratory symptoms of an exacerbation rather than solely physiological, or causative factors. The strongest predictor of a patient's future exacerbation frequency remains the number of exacerbations they have had in the prior year.[289] It is recognized that these patients form a moderately stable phenotype, although some studies have shown that a significant proportion of patients change their exacerbation frequency especially with worsening FEV$_1$.[292]

Other factors that have been associated with an increased risk of acute exacerbations and/or severity of exacerbations include an increase in the ratio of the pulmonary artery to aorta cross sectional dimension (i.e., ratio > 1),[293] a greater percentage of emphysema or airway wall thickness[294] measured by chest CT imaging and the presence of chronic bronchitis.[21,295]

Vitamin D has an immune-modulating role and has been implicated in the pathophysiology of exacerbations. As with all chronic diseases vitamin D levels are lower in COPD than in health. Studies have shown that supplementation in subjects with severe deficiency results in a 50% reduction in episodes and hospital admission.[216] Therefore it is recommended that all patients hospitalized for exacerbations should be assessed and investigated for severe deficiency (<10 ng/ml or <25 nM) followed by supplementation if required.

TREATMENT OPTIONS

Treatment setting

The goals of treatment for COPD exacerbations are to minimize the negative impact of the current exacerbation and prevent the development of subsequent events.[296] Depending on the severity of an exacerbation and/or the severity of the underlying disease, an exacerbation can be managed in either the outpatient or inpatient setting. More than 80% of exacerbations are managed on an outpatient basis with pharmacological therapies including bronchodilators, corticosteroids, and antibiotics. [15,23,24]

When patients with a COPD exacerbation come to the emergency department, they should be provided with supplemental oxygen and undergo assessment to determine whether the exacerbation is life-threatening and if increased work of breathing or impaired gas exchange requires consideration for non-invasive ventilation (**see Table**). If so, healthcare providers should consider admission to the respiratory or intensive care unit of the hospital. Otherwise, the patient may be managed in the emergency department or hospital ward unit. In addition to pharmacological therapy, hospital management of exacerbations includes respiratory support (oxygen therapy, ventilation). The management of severe, but not life-threatening, exacerbations is also outlined (**see Table**).

▶ POTENTIAL INDICATIONS FOR HOSPITALIZATION ASSESSMENT*

- Severe symptoms such as sudden worsening of resting dyspnea, high respiratory rate, decreased oxygen saturation, confusion, drowsiness.
- Acute respiratory failure.
- Onset of new physical signs (e.g., cyanosis, peripheral edema).
- Failure of an exacerbation to respond to initial medical management.
- Presence of serious comorbidities (e.g., heart failure, newly occurring arrhythmias, etc.).
- Insufficient home support.

*Local resources need to be considered.

▶ MANAGEMENT OF SEVERE BUT NOT LIFE-THREATENING EXACERBATIONS*

- Assess severity of symptoms, blood gases, chest radiograph.
- Administer supplemental oxygen therapy, obtain serial arterial blood gas, venous blood gas and pulse oximetry measurements.
- Bronchodilators:
    » Increase doses and/or frequency of short-acting bronchodilators.
    » Combine short-acting beta 2-agonists and anticholinergics.
    » Consider use of long-active bronchodilators when patient becomes stable.
    » Use spacers or air-driven nebulizers when appropriate.
- Consider oral corticosteroids.
- Consider antibiotics (oral) when signs of bacterial infection are present.
- Consider noninvasive mechanical ventilation (NIV).
- At all times:
    » Monitor fluid balance.
    » Consider subcutaneous heparin or low molecular weight heparin for thromboembolism prophylaxis.
    » Identify and treat associated conditions (e.g., heart failure, arrhythmias, pulmonary embolism etc.).

*Local resources need to be considered.

The clinical presentation of COPD exacerbation is heterogeneous, thus we recommend that in **hospitalized patients** the severity of the exacerbation should be based on the patient's clinical signs and recommend the following classification.[297]

No respiratory failure: Respiratory rate: 20-30 breaths per minute; no use of accessory respiratory muscles; no changes in mental status; hypoxemia improved with supplemental oxygen given via Venturi mask 28-35% inspired oxygen (FiO$_2$); no increase in PaCO$_2$.

Acute respiratory failure – non-life-threatening: Respiratory rate: > 30 breaths per minute; using accessory respiratory muscles; no change in mental status; hypoxemia improved with supplemental oxygen via Venturi mask 25-30% FiO$_2$; hypercarbia i.e., PaCO$_2$ increased compared with baseline or elevated 50-60 mmHg.

Acute respiratory failure – life-threatening: Respiratory rate: > 30 breaths per minute; using accessory respiratory muscles; acute changes in mental status; hypoxemia not improved with supplemental oxygen via Venturi mask or requiring FiO$_2$ > 40%; hypercarbia i.e., PaCO$_2$ increased compared with baseline or elevated > 60 mmHg or the presence of acidosis (pH ≤ 7.25).

Long-term prognosis following hospitalization for COPD exacerbation is poor, with a five-year mortality rate of about 50%.[298] Factors independently associated with poor outcome include older age, lower BMI, comorbidities (e.g., cardiovascular disease or lung cancer), previous hospitalizations for COPD exacerbations, clinical severity of the index exacerbation and need for long-term oxygen therapy at discharge.[299-301] Patients characterized by a higher prevalence and severity of respiratory symptoms, poorer quality of life, worse lung function, lower exercise capacity, lower lung density and thickened bronchial walls on CT-scan are also at increased risk for a higher mortality following an acute COPD exacerbation.[302] Mortality risk may be heightened during spells of cold weather.[303]

A recent updated Cochrane review concluded that the use of COPD exacerbation action plans with a single short educational component, in conjunction with ongoing support, reduced in-hospital healthcare utilization. Such educational interventions were also found to increase the treatment of COPD exacerbations with corticosteroids and antibiotics.[304]

The three classes of medications most commonly used for COPD exacerbations are bronchodilators, corticosteroids, and antibiotics (**see Table**).

> ### ▶ KEY POINTS FOR THE MANAGEMENT OF EXACERBATIONS
>
> - Short-acting inhaled beta$_2$-agonists, with or without short-acting anticholinergics, are recommended as the initial bronchodilators to treat an acute exacerbation (**Evidence C**).
> - Systemic corticosteroids can improve lung function (FEV$_1$), oxygenation and shorten recovery time and hospitalization duration. Duration of therapy should not be more than 5-7 days (**Evidence A**).
> - Antibiotics, when indicated, can shorten recovery time, reduce the risk of early relapse, treatment failure, and hospitalization duration. Duration of therapy should be 5-7 days (**Evidence B**).
> - Methylxanthines are not recommended due to increased side effect profiles (**Evidence B**).
> - Non-invasive mechanical ventilation should be the first mode of ventilation used in COPD patients with acute respiratory failure who have no absolute contraindication because it improves gas exchange, reduces work of breathing and the need for intubation, decreases hospitalization duration and improves survival (**Evidence A**).

Respiratory support

Oxygen therapy. This is a key component of hospital treatment of an exacerbation. Supplemental oxygen should be titrated to improve the patient's hypoxemia with a target saturation of 88-92%.[305] Once oxygen is started, blood gases should be checked frequently to ensure satisfactory oxygenation without carbon dioxide retention and/or worsening acidosis. A recent study demonstrated that venous blood gas to assess bicarbonate levels and pH is accurate when compared with arterial blood gas assessment.[306] Additional data are needed to clarify the utility of venous blood gas sampling to make clinical decisions in scenarios of acute respiratory failure; most patients included had a pH > 7.30 on presentation, PCO_2 levels were dissimilar when measured by venous compared to arterial blood samples and the severity of airflow limitation was not reported.[306] Venturi masks (high-flow devices) offer more accurate and controlled delivery of oxygen than do nasal prongs.[307]

High-flow oxygen therapy by nasal cannula. High-flow oxygen (HFO) involves nasal delivery of heated and humidified oxygen via special devices (e.g., Vapotherm®, Comfort Flo®, or Optiflow®) at rates up to 8 L/min in infants and up to 60 L/min in adults.[308] In patients with acute hypoxemic respiratory failure, HFO may be an alternative to standard oxygen therapy or noninvasive positive pressure ventilation. In observational studies, HFO has been associated with decreased respiratory rate and effort, decreased work of breathing, improved gas exchange, improved lung volume, dynamic compliance, transpulmonary pressures and homogeneity. All these physiologic benefits might positively improve oxygenation and clinical outcome in ARF patients.[309] Studies to date were performed in COPD patients with very severe underlying disease that required supplemental oxygen; a randomized cross-over trial demonstrated that HFO improved oxygenation and ventilation, and decreased hypercarbia. [310,311] A systematic review of RCTs in patients with acute hypoxemic respiratory failure suggests that HFO tends to reduce intubation rate, but did not meet statistical significance compared with conventional oxygen therapy or NIV, and had no effect on mortality.[312] Several randomized controlled trials have also studied the use of HFO therapy to reduced hypercapnia and improved health-related quality of life in patients with stable hypercapnic COPD.[313-315] There is a need for well-designed, randomized, multicenter trials to study the effects of HFO in both acute and chronic hypoxemic/hypercarbic respiratory failure in COPD patients.

Ventilatory Support. Some patients need immediate admission to the respiratory care or intensive care unit (ICU) **(see Table)**. Admission of patients with severe exacerbations to intermediate or special respiratory care units may be appropriate if adequate personnel skills and equipment exist to identify and manage acute respiratory failure. Ventilatory support in an exacerbation can be provided by either noninvasive (nasal or facial mask) or invasive (oro-tracheal tube or tracheostomy) ventilation. Respiratory stimulants are not recommended for acute respiratory failure.[316]

▶ **INDICATIONS FOR RESPIRATORY OR MEDICAL INTENSIVE CARE UNIT ADMISSION***

- Severe dyspnea that responds inadequately to initial emergency therapy.
- Changes in mental status (confusion, lethargy, coma).
- Persistent or worsening hypoxemia (PaO2 < 5.3 kPa or 40mmHg) and/or severe/worsening respiratory acidosis (pH < 7.25) despite supplemental oxygen and noninvasive ventilation.
- Need for invasive mechanical ventilation.
- Hemodynamic instability - need for vasopressors.

*Local resources need to be considered.

Noninvasive mechanical ventilation. The use of noninvasive mechanical ventilation (NIV) is preferred over invasive ventilation (intubation and positive pressure ventilation) as the initial mode of ventilation to treat acute respiratory failure in patients hospitalized for acute exacerbations of COPD. NIV has been studied in RCTs showing a success rate of 80-85%.[225,317-320] NIV has been shown to improve oxygenation and acute respiratory acidosis i.e., NIV increases pH and decreases PaCO2. NIV also decreases respiratory rate, work of breathing and the severity of breathlessness but also decreases complications such as ventilator associated pneumonia, and length of hospital stay. More importantly, mortality and intubation rates are reduced by this intervention.[318,321-323] Once patients improve and can tolerate at least 4 hours of unassisted breathing, NIV can be directly discontinued without any need for a "weaning" period.[324] The indications for NIV[320] are summarized in the **Table**.

Invasive mechanical ventilation. The indications for initiating invasive mechanical ventilation during an exacerbation are shown in the **Table**, and include failure of an initial trial of NIV.[325]

> ### ▶ INDICATIONS FOR INVASIVE MECHANICAL VENTILATION
>
> - Unable to tolerate NIV or NIV failure.
> - Status post - respiratory or cardiac arrest.
> - Diminished consciousness, psychomotor agitation inadequately controlled by sedation.
> - Massive aspiration or persistent vomiting.
> - Persistent inability to remove respiratory secretions.
> - Severe hemodynamic instability without response to fluids and vasoactive drugs.
> - Severe ventricular or supraventricular arrhythmias.
> - Life-threatening hypoxemia in patients unable to tolerate NIV.

Hospital discharge and follow-up

The cause, severity, impact, treatment and time course of exacerbations varies from patient to patient and facilities in the community, and healthcare systems, differ from country to country. Accordingly, there are no standards that can be applied to the timing and nature of discharge. When features related to re-hospitalization and mortality have been studied, defects in perceived optimal management have been identified including spirometric assessment and arterial blood gas analysis.[326] Mortality relates to patient age, the presence of acidotic respiratory failure, the need for ventilatory support and comorbidities including anxiety and depression (**see Table**).[327]

DISCHARGE CRITERIA AND RECOMMENDATIONS FOR FOLLOW-UP

- Full review of all clinical and laboratory data.
- Check maintenance therapy and understanding.
- Reassess inhaler technique.
- Ensure understanding of withdrawal of acute medications (steroids and/or antibiotics).
- Assess need for continuing any oxygen therapy.
- Provide management plan for comorbidities and follow-up.
- Ensure follow-up arrangements: early follow-up < 4weeks, and late follow-up < 12weeks as indicated.
- All clinical or investigational abnormalities have been identified.

 1 – 4 WEEKS FOLLOW-UP

- Evaluate ability to cope in his/her usual environment.
- Review and understanding treatment regimen.
- Reassessment of inhaler techniques.
- Reassess need for long-term oxygen.
- Document the capacity to do physical activity and activities of daily living.
- Document symptoms: CAT or mMRC.
- Determine status of comorbidities.

 12 – 16 WEEKS FOLLOW-UP

- Evaluate ability to cope in his/her usual environment.
- Review understanding treatment regimen.
- Reassessment of inhaler techniques.
- Reassess need for long-term oxygen.
- Document the capacity to do physical activity and activities of daily living.
- Measure spirometry: FEV_1.
- Document symptoms: CAT or mMRC.
- Determine status of comorbidities.

Prevention of exacerbations

After an acute exacerbation, appropriate measures for prevention of further exacerbations should be initiated (**see Table**).

47

INTERVENTIONS THAT REDUCE THE FREQUENCY OF COPD EXACERBATIONS	
INTERVENTION CLASS	INTERVENTION
Bronchodilators	LABAs
	LAMAs
	LABA + LAMA
Corticosteroid-containing regimens	LABA + ICS
	LABA + LAMA + ICS
Anti-inflammatory (non-steroid)	Roflumilast
Anti-infectives	Vaccines
	Long Term Macrolides
Mucoregulators	N-acetylcysteine
	Carbocysteine
Various others	Smoking Cessation
	Rehabilitation
	Lung Volume Reduction
	Vitamin D

COPD AND COMORBIDITIES

OVERALL KEY POINTS:

- *COPD often coexists with other diseases (comorbidities) that may have a significant impact on disease course.*

- *In general, the presence of comorbidities should not alter COPD treatment and comorbidities should be treated per usual standards regardless of the presence of COPD.*

- *Lung cancer is frequently seen in patients with COPD and is a main cause of death.*

- *Cardiovascular diseases are common and important comorbidities in COPD.*

- *Osteoporosis and depression/anxiety are frequent, important comorbidities in COPD, are often under-diagnosed, and are associated with poor health status and prognosis.*

- *Gastroesophageal reflux (GERD) is associated with an increased risk of exacerbations and poorer health status.*

- *When COPD is part of a multimorbidity care plan, attention should be directed to ensure simplicity of treatment and to minimize polypharmacy.*

REFERENCES

The full list of references for this pocket guide can be found online at: www.goldcopd.org/pocketguidereferences

Made in the USA
Middletown, DE
26 April 2021